THE PRACTICAL BIBLIOGRAPHER

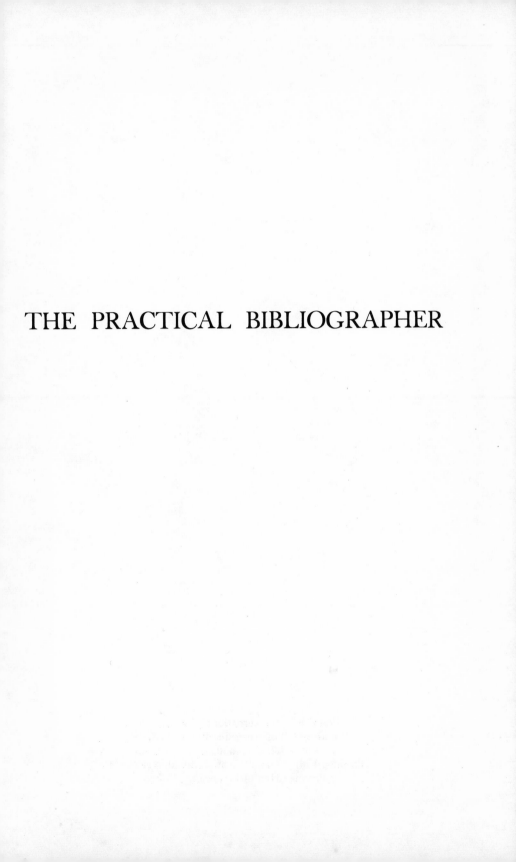

Prentice-Hall International, Inc., *London*
Prentice-Hall of Australia, Pty. Ltd., *Sydney*
Prentice-Hall of Canada, Ltd., *Toronto*
Prentice-Hall of India Private Limited, *New Delhi*
Prentice-Hall of Japan, Inc., *Tokyo*

THE

PRACTICAL

BIBLIOGRAPHER

Martha L. Hackman

John F. Kennedy Memorial Library
California State College at Los Angeles

PRENTICE-HALL, INC.
Englewood Cliffs, New Jersey

© 1970 by Prentice-Hall, Inc., Englewood Cliffs, N.J.

C13-687459-2
P13-687442-8

Library of Congress Catalog Card Number 73–102281

Printed in the United States of America

Current Printing (last digit):
10 9 8 7 6 5 4 3 2 1

For Polly

PREFACE

This is a book for the apprentice scholar. It assumes that he has chosen
his field of major concentration and that he is preparing for serious independent work in that field. It offers to help him acquire, as part of his
scholar's equipment, a background in general bibliography. It may serve
as a text wherever an introduction to bibliography is needed, particularly
in those courses which introduce the student to the methods and literature
of his own discipline.

More specifically, *The Practical Bibliographer* seeks to introduce some
of the classes of bibliography which underlie scholarship: national and
trade bibliography, the bibliography of government publications, union lists
and catalogs, as well as general subject bibliography. It examines the
functions and structure of scholarly bibliography and some of its common
forms: the retrospective bibliography, the current bibliography, the review
of research, and the guide to literature. It seeks to help the student develop
skill in documenting his own work. Finally, it hopes to give him a sense of
the continuity of scholarship through the perspective of historical bibliography.

It has not been my intent to recommend or describe individual bibliographic works. (There is no lack of good manuals for this purpose.)
Rather I have tried to emphasize the forms which bibliography takes in
performing its principal functions, to invite the student to examine a few
representative titles, and to challenge him to explore further along lines
of his own interest. A few areas for exploration are suggested following

each chapter. Others will doubtless be indicated by students' special interests.

Georg Schneider, in his invaluable *Theory and History of Bibliography*, makes it a rule that no book should be mentioned which cannot also be shown to the student. While they are admittedly not the ideal substitute for the real book, the many facsimile pages which accompany the text allow for those occasions when examination of the actual book is not possible or practical.

My thanks are due to two colleagues, Lois Di Santo and Morris Polan, for their encouragement and generous assistance; and to the many students who, by sharing with me their bibliographic problems, have unwittingly contributed to the making of this book.

Riverside, California   M.L.H.

CONTENTS

I

WHAT IS BIBLIOGRAPHY?

*So much has already been written about everything
that you can't find out anything about it.*

—*James Thurber*[1]

Not even bibliographers agree on the meaning of the word *bibliography*. According to some it means the precise identification of books and the description of them as physical objects. This is sometimes called *descriptive bibliography*, and its practitioners are versed in the details of typography and binding, the chemical composition of paper, and the history of book manufacture. Their expertise is often in demand to establish the value of a rare book or to detect a forgery, but such matters, however fascinating, are beyond the scope of this book.[2]

In another sense bibliography is the listing of books, as well as other records, in ways that make them readily accessible. The practitioners of this type of bibliography, known as *systematic bibliography*, are the makers of lists and indexes intended to bring order to the chaos of recorded knowledge. The following chapters will discuss chiefly this type of bibliography defined as the orderly presentation of the records of human experience. The word *bibliography* will also be used to refer to the result of this process: an orderly list of references such as is often found at the end of a chapter or book.

---

[1]From "The New Vocabularianism," in *Lanterns and Lances*. Copr. © 1961 James Thurber. Published by Harper and Row, p. 120.

[2]The interested reader is referred to Richard Altick's *The Scholar Adventurers* (New York: The Macmillan Company, 1950) for some delightful accounts of bibliographic detective work.

THE BEGINNINGS OF BIBLIOGRAPHY

The need for an orderly presentation of records began to be recognized as a serious problem shortly after the invention of printing. This event so enormously multiplied the number of records available that scholars found it difficult to know what had been written. The idea of bringing together into one list all of the scholarly books of the time occurred to Conrad Gesner, a doctor of Zurich, who was to become known as the Father of Bibliography. By using what lists he could find and by scouring the great libraries of Europe, he managed to include approximately 12,000 books in his *Bibliotheca Universalis sive Catalogus Omnium Scriptorum Locupletissimus in Tribus Linguis Latina, Graeca, et Hebraica*, which he published in 1545. He arranged books by the first names of authors and provided an index grouping the books into twenty subject divisions. Ten years later he issued an appendix listing an additional 3,000 books.

Printing with movable type had been invented a mere one hundred years before Gesner compiled his list, but his diligent searching had accounted for approximately one third of the output of European presses. Although others tried, no one succeeded in listing in a single catalog all the books in the world. As Europe entered the seventeenth century, with men like Galileo, Newton, and Boyle leading the search for scientific truth, the flood of print overwhelmed the bibliographers, who were forced to place realistic limits on their work. By these limits we may trace the beginnings of the principal types of modern bibliography. Some bibliographers, like Andrew Maunsell, who in 1595 issued his *Catalogue of English Printed Books*, confined themselves to the publishing output of their own countries. In this way they not only appealed to national pride but also avoided being seriously inconvenienced by wars. Modern bibliographers, following this tradition, have developed reasonably complete national bibliographies. Another line of descent passes through the booksellers' catalogs prepared for the bookfairs that, beginning in the latter half of the sixteenth century, were held at Frankfurt and Leipzig. This line leads to the modern trade bibliography of books in print and for sale. A third type, the subject bibliography, grew slowly at first, then flowered in the nineteenth century with such great scholarly bibliographies as Emil Hübner's *Bibliographie der Klassichen Altertumswissenschaft*[3] and Sir Thomas Duffus Hardy's *Descriptive Catalogue of Materials Relating to the History of Great Britain and Ireland*.[4]

---

[3] (2d. ed.; Berlin: W. Hertz, 1889).
[4] (London: Longman, Green, Longman, & Roberts, 1862–71), 4 vols.

BIBLIOGRAPHY TODAY

Today we face a situation not unlike that which immediately followed the invention of printing. The amount of information generated and needed by our technological civilization is so great and is increasing so rapidly that it threatens to overpower us. As long ago as 1945 Vannevar Bush wrote:

> There is a growing mountain of research. But there is evidence that we are being bogged down today as specialization extends. The investigator is staggered by the findings and conclusions of thousands of other workers—conclusions which he cannot find time to grasp, much less to remember, as they appear. . . . Mendel's concept of the laws of of genetics was lost to the world for a generation because his publication did not reach the few who were capable of grasping and extending it; and this sort of catastrophe is undoubtedly being repeated all about us. . . .[5]

He went on to predict a machine that he named a memex, by means of which a scholar might record his work, step by step, leaving it to be built upon by others.

Reminiscent of the memex is the Massachusetts Institute of Technology's PROJECT MAC, an acronym variously translated as Machine Aided Cognition, Multiple Access Computer, or simply Man And Computer. Here scientists share a large computer, develop their own programs, carry on dialogue, and, with permission, use one another's files. The system and its participants have reportedly developed as a growing organism. The men exchange data and build upon each other's work, relying on the mass memory of the machine. Reports indicate, however, that users are beginning to complain of the inefficiency in finding out what the memory contains and of locating what is useful.[6] Thus we find ourselves facing the problem out of which bibliography first arose: the need to impose order on the scattered records of human experience.

BIBLIOGRAPHIES OF BIBLIOGRAPHIES

We must still rely heavily on a legacy of limited and specialized lists to cover the increasingly complex world of modern scholarship. By 1963 the num-

---

[5]"As We May Think," *Atlantic*, CLXXVI, No. 1 (1945), 101–2.
[6]R.M. Fano and F.J. Corbató. "Time-Sharing on Computers," *Scientific American*, CCXV, No. 3 (1966), 140.

ber of separately published bibliographies was well over 117,000. This is the number recorded by Theodore Besterman in the fourth edition of his *A World Bibliography of Bibliographies.*[7] In four large volumes he lists bibliographies of all times, on all subjects, limiting himself, however, to those published in western languages and issued as separate books or pamphlets. A fifth volume consists of an index to the authors, editors, translators, series, and, in the case of anonymous works, to the titles of these bibliographies.

On a typical page from this work, shown in Figure 1, the subjects range from *Cacao* to *Caddos*, and the number of items, shown by a numeral in brackets following each entry, ranges from 11 to 2,700. Cross-references direct the reader from *Cabinet-making* to *Carpentry* and from *Cables* to *Telegraphy and Telephony.* It is a veritable monument of bibliography. Even so indefatigable a bibliographer as Mr. Besterman, however, finds it difficult to keep up with the quantity of bibliographies now being produced. With his third edition, in 1955, he tried unsuccessfully to conclude this work. He has said that the present edition, which contains about 30,000 additional titles, is the final one.

The Bibliographic Index,[8] on the other hand, records new bibliographies as they are issued, whether they appear as separate books or pamphlets or as lists accompanying other works. Thousands of new books and periodicals are continually searched for bibliographies to include in this index. The *Bibliographic Index,* which began in 1937, is issued twice a year in paperbound form. These seminannual issues are then cumulated (*i.e.,* combined) and eventually form a permanent file of bound volumes, each covering several years. The page from this work shown in Figure 2 illustrates three types of bibliographies: the list of a few pages included within a larger work (any of the items under the subject *Machiavelli*), the list in a periodical (the item by Garretson under *Machinery—Maintenance and Repair*), and the separate bibliography (the list by Balz and Stanwell under the subject *Machine Translating*).

The bibliography of bibliographies is not always the most direct route to information. It has its uses, however, as a means of gaining entrance to the literature of an obscure or limited topic or one not adequately covered in the usual bibliographies. It has been mentioned here because it offers an introduction to the field of bibliography and because nothing so clearly demonstrates the extent of the bibliographic problem. However much he may yearn for the simplicity of a universal list, the scholar who lacks a knowledge of the realities of bibliography runs the risk of overlooking an

---

[7]Theodore Besterman, *A World Bibliography of Bibliographies*, 4th ed. (Lausanne: Societas Bibliographica, 1965–66), 5 vols.

[8]*Bibliographic Index: A Cumulative Bibliography of Bibliographies,* 1937–date (New York: The H.W. Wilson Co., 1945–date).

C

Caamaño, José Francisco Juan Maria, *in religion* Diego José.

SERAFIN DE AUSEJO, Reseña bibliográfica de las obras impresas del beato Diego José de Cádiz (1743–1801). Madrid 1947. pp.lii.332. [282.]

Caballa. *see* Kaballa.

Cabannes, Camille.

[C. CABANNES], Titres et travaux scientifiques du dr C. Cabannes. 1901. pp.60. [54.]

Cabell, James Branch.

MERLE [DE VORE] JOHNSON, A bibliographic check-list of the works of James Branch Cabell, 1904–1921. New York 1921. pp.28. [25.]
250 copies printed.

GUY HOLT, A bibliography of the writings of James Branch Cabell. The centaur bibliographies [of modern american authors] (no.3): Philadelphia 1924. pp.73. [200.]
500 copies printed.

I[SIDORE] R[OSENBAUM] BRUSSEL, A bibliography of the writings of James Branch Cabell. The centaur bibliographies [of modern american authors] (no.11): Philadelphia 1932. pp.132. [300.]
350 copies printed.

FRANCES JOAN BREWER, James Branch Cabell. A bibliography of his writings, biography and criticism. Charlottesville, Va. 1957. pp.[ii].206. [533.]
— — Part II. Notes on the Cabell collections at the university of Virginia, by Matthew J. Bruscóli. 1957. pp.178. [750.]

Cabinet-making. *see* Carpentry.

Cables. *see* Telegraphy and telephony.

Cabot, John and Sebastian.

GEORGE PARKER WINSHIP, Cabot bibliography. [Providence, R.I.] 1897. pp.71. [300.]
— — [another edition]. 1900. pp.liii.181. [579.]

Cacao.

LIST of references on cacao (cocoa) and chocolate cultivation, manufacture and uses. Library of Congress: [Washington] 1921. ff.10. [123.]*

1077

— Additional references [&c.]. 1933. ff.7. [86.]*

WITCH-BROOM diesease of cacao. Science library: Bibliographical series (no.264): 1936. ff.4. [74.]*

INSECTS infesting cacao beans, including their life history and methods of control. References covering the period 1930–1938. Science library: Bibliographical series (no.494): 1939. ff.5. [70.]*

WOLF MUELLER, Bibliographie des kakao, seiner geschichte, kultur, verwendung, verarbeitung, wirtschaftlichen bedeutung. Hamburg 1951. pp.[ii].120. [2700.]

PUBLICATIONS on cacao. Imperial college of tropical agriculture: St Augustine, Trinidad 1955. pp.[5]. [100.]*

BIBLIOGRAPHIE des travaux récents effectués sur le cacaoyer. Commission du Pacifique sud: Circulaire d'information technique (no.30): [Nouméa] 1957. pp.[i].33. [102.]*

Cáceres.

ANTONIO C. FLORIANO, Documentación histórica del archivo municipal de Cáceres. Cáceres.
i. 1217–1504. 1934. pp.280. [378.]

Cachera, René.

[R. CACHERA], Exposé des titres et des travaux scientifiques du dr René Cachera. 1939. pp.155. [97.]

Cactus.

SELECT list of publications in english on cacti in the Science library. Science library: Bibliographical series (no.47): [1932]. single sheet. [11.]*

Cadaval, family of.

VIRGÍNIA [ROBERTS] RAU and MARIA FERNANDA GOMES DA SILVA, Os manuscritos do arquivo da casa de Cadaval respeitantes ao Brasil. Acta universitatis conimbrigensis: [Coimbra] 1955–1958. pp.xv.543+[iii].483. [1118.]

Caddos.

KENNETH LAWRENCE BEAUDOIN, The Caddos. A selected reading list . . . on the Caddo Indians of northern Louisiana and southern Arkansas. Jasper 1951. ff.[7]. [75.]*

1078

FIGURE 1. BESTERMAN'S A WORLD BIBLIOGRAPHY OF BIBLIOGRAPHIES [Theodore Besterman, *A World Bibliography of Bibliographies* (4th ed.; Lusanne: Societas Bibliographica, 1965–66) Vol. 1, col. 1077 and 1078. Used by permission of the author.]

BIBLIOGRAPHIC INDEX 1963—1965 411

MACHIAVELLI, Niccolò—*Continued*
Gilbert, Felix. Machiavelli and Guicciardini; politics and history in sixteenth-cent. Florence. Princeton univ. press '65 p316-30 annot
Machiavelli, Niccolò. Prince; tr. with an introd. by A. Robert Caponigri. (Gateway ed. 6081) Regnery '63 p 147-8
Raab, Felix. English face of Machiavelli; a changing interpretation, 1500-1700; with a foreword by Hugh Trevor-Roper. (Studies in political history) Univ. of Toronto press '64 p273-83 annot

MACHINE language. See Programming languages (electronic computers)

MACHINE parts
IAkovlev, Vsevolod Fedorovich, and InTUtin, Ivan Sergeevich. Measurements for stresses in machine components; tr. from the Russian by J. J. Cornish; tr. ed. by M. L. Meyer. Pergamon '64 p 130-2

MACHINE shop practice
Hague. Technisch documentatie- en informatiecentrum voor de krijgsmacht. Werkplaatstechniek; literatuuroverzicht. The center. See numbers
Niebel, Benjamin W. Machine shop-job type. (Small business bibliog. no69) U.S. Small business adm. '64 12p
See also
Drilling and boring (metal making, etc)
Stamping

MACHINE shops
Mystkowski, Andrzej, and Winiarski, Bolesław. Elektronika obrabiarkowa. Państwowe wydawn. techniczne '61 p337-41
See also
School shops

MACHINE tools
Galloway, D. F. Machine tool research, design, and utilization. Inst Mech Eng Proc 175:147 '61
International machine tool design and research conference. Advances in machine tool design and research; proceedings of the 3d [-5th] Conference, 1962[-1964] ed. by S. A. Tobias and F. Koenigsberger. Pergamon '63-'65 3v incl bibliog
Rolt, Lionel Thomas Caswell. Short history of machine tools. M.I.T. press '65 p245-7
See also
Metal cutting
Tool steel

Hydraulic drive

Khaĭmovich, E. M. Hydraulic control of machine tools; tr. by O. Tedder; tr. ed. by K. Foster. Pergamon '65 p561-5

Numerical control

American society of tool and manufacturing engineers. Numerical control in manufacturing. Frank W. Wilson, editor-in-chief. McGraw '63 incl bibliog
Bell, R. Survey of the techniques evolved for the measurement of position in numerically controlled machine tools. Brit Inst Radio Eng J 25:222-3 Mr '63

MACHINE translating
Akhmanova, O. S. and others. Exact methods in linguistic research; tr. from the Russian by David G. Hays and Dolores V. Mohr. Univ. of Calif. press '63 incl bibliog
Balz, Charles F. and Stanwood, Richard H. Literature on information retrieval and machine translation. Int. business machines corp. '62 117p
Bar-Hillel, Yehoshua. Language and information; sel. essays on their theory and application. (Addison-Wesley ser. in logic; ADIWES int. ser) Addison-Wesley '64 p373-8
Bryce, Barbara Ann. Literature of machine translation; an annot. bibliography. Autonetics div, North Am. aviation, inc. '62 1v
Harper, Kenneth Eugene, and others. Studies in machine translation; bibliog. of Russian scientific articles. (Memorandum RM-3610-PR) Rand corp. '63 97p
Walkowicz, Josephine L. Bibliography of foreign developments in machine translation and information processing. (Technical note 193) U.S. Nat. bur. of standards '63 191p

MACHINERY
See also
Agricultural machinery
Bearings
Calenders
Electric machinery
Friction
Gearing
Governors (machinery)
Hydraulic machinery
Locomotives
Lubrication and lubricants
Machine parts
Machine tools
Packing (mechanical engineering)
Replacement of industrial equipment
Turbines
Wood chipping machines

Foundations

Major, Sándor. Berechnung und planung von maschinen- und turbinenfundamenten; schwingungen im bau- und verkehrswesen. Verlag der Ungarischen Akad. der wissenschaften '61 p833-7

Maintenance and repair

Garretson, R. C. Preventive maintenance scheduling with punched cards. Lub Eng 19:20 Ja '63

Parts

See Machine parts

MACHINERY, Automatic
Phillips, R. S. and Davison, G. N. Mechanizing the postal service. Inst Mech Eng Proc 177 no8:216-17 '63
Shaumian, G. A. Automaten [übers. aus dem russischen: K. Stubenrauch] 2d rev & enl ed Verlag Technik '61 p749-53
See also
Automation
Vending machines

MACHINERY, Kinematics of
Beyer, Rudolf. Kinematic synthesis of mechanisms; tr. from the German by H. Kuenzel. McGraw '63 p332-45
Freudenstein, F. and Primrose, E. J. F. Geared five-bar motion. A S M E Trans serE 30:169 Je '63
Hain, Kurt. Angewandte getriebelehre. 2d rev & enl ed VDI-verlag '61 p521-84
Yang, A. T. Harmonic analysis of spherical four-bar mechanisms. A S M E Trans serE 29:687-8 D '62
See also
Rolling contact

MACHINERY and civilization. See Technology and civilization

MACHINES and the library. See Mechanization of library processes

MCIVER, John, 1764-1828
Tennessee. State library and archives, Nashville. Manuscript section. McIver collection. (Its Registers, no4) The library '62 9p

MCKILLOP, Alan Dugald, 1892-
Camden, Charles Carroll, ed. Restoration and eighteenth-century literature; essays in honor of Alan Dugald McKillop [contributors: Rae Blanchard and others] pub. for William Marsh Rice univ; bibliog. comp. by Stuart Wilson] Univ. of Chicago press '63 p429-35

MAC-LEAN Y ESTENÓS, Roberto, 1904-
Mac-Lean y Estenós, Roberto. Sociología del Perú. (Colección Monografías sociológicas iberoamericanas) Inst. de investigaciones sociales, Univ. nacional de México '59 p664-6

MCNABB, Vincent Joseph, 1868-1943
Auth, Charles Robert. Bibliography of the published writings of Vincent Joseph McNabb, O. P. 3d ed Dominican house of studies '63 72p

MCNEILL, John Thomas, 1885-
Shepherd, Holley M. Bio-bibliography of John Thomas McNeill. Andover-Harvard theological lib. '60 p21-36

MACROMOLECULES
Ingram, Vernon M. Biosynthesis of macromolecules. (Biology teaching monograph ser) Benjamin '65 incl bibliog
Vollmert, Bruno. Grundriss der makromolekularen chemie. Springer '62 p444-78

MACSWINEY, Terence Joseph, 1879-1920
Fox, Moireen. Terence MacSwiney, by Moirin Chavasse; with a foreword by Daniel Corkery. Clonmore & Reynolds '61 p 10

MADAGASCAR
Decary, R. Chronique de l'histoire d'outre-mer: Madagascar (1956-1960) R Française Hist Outre-Mer 49 no3-4:438-72 '62 (i.e.Ja '64)
Stratton, Arthur. Great red island. Scribner '64 p351-5

Antiquities

Vérin, P. Rétrospective et problèmes de l'archéologie à Madagascar. Asian Perspect 6 no 1-2:210-18 '62

MADISON COUNTY, Kentucky
Jillson, Willard Rouse. Bibliography of Madison County, Kentucky; citations of ptd. and ms. sources touching upon its history, cartography, geology, calcite, barite, fluorite, galenite, sphalerite, oil and gas, with brief annots (1750-1963). Roberts print. co. '64 35p

FIGURE 2. BIBLIOGRAPHIC INDEX [*The Bibliographic Index* (New York: The H. W. Wilson Company, volume for 1963–65) p. 411. Used by permission of the publisher.]

important and relevant piece of work or even of duplicating work already done. The study of the orderly presentation of records has never been more necessary or more difficult. The modern scholar has more records to search and organize than his predecessors could have dreamed of. Only the mastery of bibliography can save him from drowning in his own erudition.

SUGGESTIONS FOR FURTHER INVESTIGATION

The bibliographies of bibliographies cited above are only a few examples of this kind of publication. No doubt you will discover many others in your own field of interest. The following suggestions are intended as starting points for your investigations.

   I. One highly useful bibliography of the bibliographies of a geographic region is Raymond Tanghe's *Bibliography of Canadian Bibliographies* (Toronto: University of Toronto Press, 1960). Is there a bibliography of bibliographies of a country or region in which you are interested? If not, you may wish to compile one.
  II. Henry P. Beers' *Bibliographies in American History*, rev. ed. (New York: The H.W. Wilson Co., 1942) is a bibliography of bibliographies of a particular subject field. Is there a bibliography of bibliographies of a subject in which you are interested? If not, you may want to compile one.
 III. Can you identify[9] a bibliography of bibliographies of persons? How would this be useful to you?
  IV. Can you identify[9] a general bibliography of bibliographies other than Besterman or the *Bibliographic Index*? What would be its usefulness to you?

References for the preceding problems

The following sources will suggest other bibliographies of bibliographies for investigation. See also the card catalog of your library under the subject.

Bibliography—Bibliography

Collison, Robert L., *Bibliographies, Subject and National.* 2d. ed. New York: Hafner Publishing Co., Inc., 1962.

---

[9]To identify a book, give author's name (if any), title, publisher, place, and date of publication.

To identify a periodical or other publication issued serially, give title, date of publication, place of publication, publisher.

Malclès, Louise-Noëlle, *Les Sources du Travail Bibliographique*. Genève: E. Droz; Lille: Giard, 1950–58. 4 vols.

Taylor, Archer, *A History of Bibliographies of Bibliographies*. New Brunswick, N.J.: Scarecrow Press, Incorporated, 1955.

Winchell, Constance M., *Guide to Reference Books*. 8th ed. Chicago: Amercian Library Association, 1967. This is continued by a *First Supplement, 1965–1966*, compiled by Eugene P. Sheehy (Chicago: American Library Association, 1968).

II

CURRENT NATIONAL
AND TRADE BIBLIOGRAPHY

Hence every year our books in torrents run.
—Nicholas Boileau-Despreaux[1]

The nearest approach yet achieved to a universal register of books may be found in the national and trade bibliographies of individual countries. A national bibliography may be defined as a comprehensive list of works published in a country, or related to a country, or in the language of a country. A trade bibliography, on the other hand, is a list of books in print or for sale, usually compiled by a publisher or a bookseller. The line between national bibliography and comprehensive trade bibliography is not always distinct. However, it is not necessary to draw it too sharply because the service both perform for the scholar is essentially the same: they supply an official census of published works against which he may check his references when necessary. Has a particular book actually been published? How many pages does it have? Does it form part of a series? What is the spelling of the author's name? These questions and others like them may be answered by referring to the official description of the book. The earliest description, and therefore the one most likely to be accurate, will have appeared in the current national or trade bibliography of the book's native country at the time of publication.

---

[1]*Satire 9*, line 105.

9

CURRENT LISTS: THE UNITED STATES

Before Publication

Any book published in the United States may be listed several times. The first mention will very likely occur several months before publication in *Forthcoming Books*,[2] a bimonthly list of new books, including those scheduled for publication within five months. Books are listed under the names of their authors and titles (Figure 3). In the *Subject Guide to Forthcoming Books* they appear also under their subjects. The price, publisher, and date of publication are given, along with certain coded information (*e.g., J* to indicate a juvenile book). For the book not yet published this is a tentative listing, subject to change. After publication the book continues to be listed in *Forthcoming Books* until it is included in the annual edition of another trade bibliography, *Books in Print*,[3] where it will be listed as long as it is available for sale from its publisher.

At the Time Of Publication

Upon publication a book will probably be included in the Weekly Record section of *Publishers' Weekly*,[4] a journal that carries articles and news of interest to the book trade in addition to its regular list of new books. The headnote in Figure 4 calls this a "conscientious listing of current American book publication," but notes certain classes of books that are not included.[5] The list is arranged by names of authors or, if no author is evident, by titles. (For examples of title entries see *Allan Kaprow, American Junior Colleges,* and *Annual Review of Nuclear Science*.) Near the right-hand margin of the first line of each entry (except in the case of fiction) is the Dewey Decimal Classification number, included for the benefit of the many libraries that use this list when ordering books. The title is given next, followed by the imprint.[6] Both the title and the imprint are taken from the title page of the publication, with any additional information enclosed in brackets, (*e.g.,* [1967,c. 1937], indicating that the date of publication and the date

---

[2]*Forthcoming Books* (New York: R.R. Bowker Company, 1966–date).

[3]*Books in Print* (New York: R.R. Bowker Company, 1948–date).

[4]*Publishers' Weekly* (New York: R.R. Bowker Company, 1872–date).

[5]Subscription books are those sold by soliciting individual orders, e.g., certain encyclopedias. *New printing* refers to the issuing of additional copies without any change from the previous printing. In a *reissue, reprint,* or *revised* or *new edition* changes are made in the format or the text.

[6]The imprint consists of the place of publication, the publisher, and the date of publication.

Author Index

A C I Committee 116, ed. Cement & Concrete Terminology. Nov. 1967. 3.00. AmConcrete.

Aarons. E. S. Assignment: Marta Tirana. Mar 28, 1968. 0.50. GM. Fawcett World.

Aarons. E. S. Assignment: Moon Girl. Sep 28, 1967. 0.50. GM. Fawcett World.

Aarons. E. S. Dark Destiny. Jun 1, 1968. 0.60. Macfadden.

Aarons. E. S. Say It with Murder. Jan, 1968. 0.60. Macfadden.

Abbe. G. Funeral. Nov 13, 1967. 4.95. Horizon.

Abbey, E. Desert Solitaire. Jan 29, 1968. 5.95. McGraw.

Abbey, S. Automobile Workshop Practice. 2nd ed. Sep 14, 1967. 4.25. Soccer.

Abbey, S. Book of the B. M. C. Minis. Nov 7, 1967. 2.00. Soccer.

Abbey, S. Book of the Morris Oxford & Cowley. 4th ed. Nov 21, 1967. 2.50. Soccer.

Abbey, S. Book of the Vauxhall Victor. 2nd ed. Sep 11, 1967. 2.50. Soccer.

Abbot, C. C. Life & Letters of George Darley: Poet & Critic. Jun, 1967. 5.60;4.76. Oxford U Pr.

Abbott, M. Freedmen's Bureau in South Carolina, 1865-1872. Nov 25, 1967. 5.00. U of NC Pr.

A------- Whispering Gables. Feb 15, 1968. 0.50.

Abrahams, R. G. Peoples of Greater Unyamwezi, Tanzania. Feb 27, 1968. 4.25. Intl Pubns Serv.

Abrahams, W., ed. Prize Stories 1968 The O. Henry Awards. Mar 1, 1968. 5.95. Doubleday.

Abramoff, P. & Thomson., R. Investigations of Cells & Organisms: A Laboratory Study in Biology. (Elhi). Dec, 1967. 4.24. Fortress.

Abramovitz, J. Adult Education American History Study Lessons. 9 Bks. Sep, 1967. 4.77. Follett Educ.

Abramovitz, J. Adult Education Study Lessons in Our Nation's History. 8 Bks. Sep, 1967. 4.26. Follett Educ.

Abrams, M. H. et al. eds. Norton Anthology of English Literature. Vol. 1. rev. ed. Feb 29, 1968. 7.65 ea.;5.95x ea. Norton.

— — Norton Anthology of English Literature. Major Authors Edition. rev. ed. Apr 15, 1968. 9.45;7.45x. Norton.

Abrokossow., D. I. Revelations of a Russian Diplomat: The Memoirs of Dmitrii I Abrikossow. Apr, 1968. 6.95;2.95 U of Wash Pr.

Abshire, D. M. South Rejects a Prophet: The Life of Senator D. M. Key, 1824-1900. Dec 27, 1967. 5.95. Praeger.

Accas, G. & Eckstein, J. H. How to Protect Your Child. Jun 1968. 1.00. Escandess

Title Index

A B C - T V Word & Picture Guide to Winter Olympics. 1968. Mehlman, B. Il. by Riger. R. Jan 10. 1968. 1.00. Rutledge.

A B C: An Alphabet Book. Photos by T. Matthiesen. (J). May 1, 1968. 2.50. Platt.

A B C Book. (J). rev. ed. Sep. 1967. 1.00. Golden Pr.

A B C Europe Production. 1967. 8th ed. Feb 2. 1968. 35.00. Intl Pubns Serv.

A B C Winter Olympics. 1968. Mehlman, B. Feb. 1968. 1.00. G&D.

A. B. Frost Book. Reed, H. M. Il. by Frost. A. B. Oct 15. 1967. 20.00. C E Tuttle.

A. B. Guthrie Jr. Ford, T. Jun 1, 1968. 1.00. Steck-V.

A-D Copyfitter. Ed. by Gottschall, E. rev. ed. Apr, 1968. 3.50. Art Dir.

A-Eighteen. Taylor, T. Sep 22, 1967. 5.95. Crown.

A. H. Reed: An Autobiography. Reed. A. H. Feb 12. 1968. 6.00. Tri-Ocean.

A Is for Alphabet. Cathy et al Il. by Suyeoka, G. (J). Feb 12, 1968. 3.75;3.52. Lothrop.

A Is for Always: An A B C Book. Anglund, J. W. Il. by Anglund. J. W. (J). Mar 20, 1968. 1.95. HB&W.

A M-F M-T V Alignment. Middleton. R. G. Nov 1, 1967. 3.50. Sams

Abnormal Sexual Development. Federman, D. D. Sep. 1967. 8.75. Saunders.

Aboard & Abroad. 1968. Olson, H. S. Nov. 1967. 6.95. Lippincott.

Abortion on Trial. Shaw. R. Apr 30, 1968. 4.95. Pflaum.

About Bananas. Russell. S. P. Il. by Rogers, C. (J). Apr 1. 1968. 2.50;1.88. Melmont.

About Britain. Harris, K. Photos by M. Peto. Apr 16. 1968. 10.00. HM.

About Farm Helpers. Payton, E. Il. by Ornstein. P. (J). rev. ed. Oct, 1967. 2.50;1.88. Melmont.

About Farm Helpers. Roth, H. L. (J). rev. ed. Sep. 1967. 2.50; 1.88 PLB. Humanities.

About Friendly Helpers for Health & Safety. Hoffman, E & Hefflefinger. J. P. Irwin (J). rev. ed. Oct 1, 1967. 2.50;1.88. Melmont.

About Going Away. F 1. Ikeda, H. Oct, 1967; 2.90. Stanwix.

About Hoping. Allemand, E. Sep 29, 1967. 0.75 Pflaum.

About Lobsters. Prudden, T. M. rev. ed. Apr 3, 1968. 6.95. Wheelwright.

About Paper. Dean, A. Il. by O'Malley, R. (J). Apr 1. 1968. 2.50;1.88. Melmont.

About Postmen. Hastings, E. For complete list. see

WEEKLY RECORD

A conscientious listing of current American book publication. Each entry, except those marked with an asterisk (*), represents Library of Congress cataloging, with the published price added and (as required) the address of the publisher, a brief annotation, etc. A dagger (†) before an entry indicates that the original LC cataloging was updated or revised by PW. Binding is cloth unless otherwise indicated. Height of binding is given in centimeters. Where two dimensions are given, the second is width. The annotations are intended to place, not judge, the books and they have been prepared so far as possible from actual examination of the finished books. Not included in these listings are: federal and other government publications; subscription books; dissertations; new printings (as distinct from reprints, reissues, and revised or new editions); quarterlies, serials, and other periodicals; pamphlets under 49 pages; and specialized publications (catalogs, telephone books, calendars, etc.) of a transitory nature or intended as advertising.

ADLER, Hans A.   711/.7
*Sector and project planning in transporta-
tion* [by] Hans A. Adler, [Washington, Intl.
Bank for Reconstruction and Development];
dist. Hopkins [1967] x, 78p. 23cm. (World
Bank staff occasional papers, no. 4) Bibl.
[HE148.5.A3] 67-28574 pap., 1.50
1. Transportation. 2. Underdeveloped areas.
I. International Bank for Reconstruction
and Development. II. Title. (Series)

AESCHYLUS   882.1
Complete plays. Tr. into English rhyming
verse with commentaries and notes by Gilbert Murray. London, Allen & Unwin [19-
52] 266p. 19cm. Contents.—The suppli-
ant women.—The Persians.—The   seven
against Thebes.—Prometheus bound.—The
Oresteia.—The Agamemnon.—The Choeph-
oroe.—The Eumenides. [PA3827.A53] 54-
15465 4.00
1. Murray, Gilbert, 1866- tr.
Reissued. American distributor: Oxford
Univ. Pr.

ALLAN KAPROW; an exhibition   759.13
sponsored by the Art Alliance of the Pasa-
dena Art Museum. [Pasadena, Calif., Pasa-
dena Art Museum, 1967] 53p. illus. 26cm.
Includes a catalog of an exhibition at the
Pasadena Art Museum, Sept. 15-Oct. 22,
1967; Washington University, St. Louis,
Feb. 1-Mar. 3, 1968; University of Texas,
Austin, Mar. 17-Apr. 28, 1968. Bibl. [N65-
37.K27A7] 67-68442 pap., 3.50, spiral bdg.
1. Kaprow, Allan. I. Pasadena. Art Museum.
Art Alliance. II. Pasadena. Art Museum.
III. Washington University, St. Louis. IV.
Texas. University
Publishers address: 46 North Los Robles
Ave., Pasadena, Calif.

ALLEN, Katharine M.   910.4
Foreign Service diary, by Katharine M.
Allen. Washington. Potomac Bks., 1967. x,
285p. map (on lining papers) 21cm. [G469.
A214] 67-29977 4.50
1. Voyages and travels. I. Title.
Account of life in overseas posts as exper-
ienced by the wife of a Foreign Service
officer.

*ALLEN, T. Ben   FIC
The man went over the mountain. Philadelphia, Dorrance [1967,i.e.1968] 373p. 20½
cm. 5.00

AMERICAN Institute of   574/.071/17
    Biological Sciences
*Directory of bioscience departments in the
United States and Canada.* Comp. under the
direction of J. David Lockard. New York,
Reinhold [1967] xvi, 672p. 26cm. [QH319.
A5A52] 67-30533 pap., 8.50
1. Biology — Study and teaching — U. S.
— Direct. 2. Biology — Study and teaching
—Canada — Direct. I. Lockard, J. David,
comp. II, Title.

*AMERICAN junior colleges.   378.73
7th ed. Washington. Amer. Council on Education [1967] v. illus., maps. 25cm. Pub. by
a coop. arrangement between Amer. Assn.
of Jr. Colls. and the council as a companion
vol. to American universities and colleges.
Eds.: 1940. W.C. Eells. — 1948- J.P. Bogue.
1967- E.J. Gleazer. Jr., assoc. ed.; P.L.
Houts [L901.A53] 40-33685 14.00
1. Junior colleges — Direct. I. Eells. Walter
Crosby. 1886- Ed. II. Bogue. Jesse Parker,
1889- III. Gleazer, Edmund J., ed. IV.
American Council on Education. V. American Association of Junior Colleges.

AMERICAN Society for   665/.5385
    Testing and Materials. Committee D-2 on
    Petroleum Products and Lubricants.
*Engine test sequences for evaluating auto-
motive lubricants for API service MC.* Philadelphia. Amer. Soc. for Testing & Materials
[1967] iv. 102p. illus. 23cm. (ASTM special
technical pubn. no. 315-C) Sponsored by
Section I on Engine Oils of Technical Div.
B on Automotive Lubricants of ASTM
Committee D-2 on Petroleum Products and
Lubricants. [TL153.5.A44 1967] 67-30484
pap., 3.00
1. Lubricating oils — Testing. 2. Automobiles
— Lubrication. I. Title. (Series: American
Society for Testing and Materials. Special
technical publication no. 315-C)

†ANNUAL review of nuclear sci-   539.705
ence. v. 17. Palo Alto. Calif., Annual Reviews. 1967. v. illus. 23cm. Vs. 1- pub. in
co-operation with the Natl. Res. Council.
Ed. 1967- F. Segre. others. [QC770.A5] 53-
995 8.50
1. Nuclear physics—Period. 2. Atomic energy—Period. 3. Radio-chemistry—Period. I.
National Research Council.

ARCOCHA. Juan, 1927-   FIC
A candle in the wind. New York. Lyle
Stuart [1967] 187p. 21cm. [PZ4.A6735-
Can] 66-16868 4.00
1. Cuba—Hist.—1959- —Fiction. I. Title.

FIGURE 4. PUBLISHERS' WEEKLY [*Publishers' Weekly* (R. R. Bowker Company). Used by permission of the publisher.]

of copyright do not appear on the title page, but were ascertained elsewhere). Then follow the number of pages, the size (in centimeters), and often a note to indicate special features, such as bibliographies. The alphanumeric symbol following the notes is the number of the book in the Library of Congress classification system. Following this is the number used to order catalog cards, then the price of the book, and finally the tracings, *i.e.*, the additional entries which might be used for this book in a library catalog. The tracings sometimes help to clarify the subject of a book when it is not obvious from the title. (See the entry for Anderson.)

Other items of bibliographic information sometimes included in the Weekly Record are the author's birth date, his death date if any (entries for Abbey, Amerine, Aptheker, Arbingast); illustrator (Abbey); series (Adler, Aptheker); edition (Arbingast); translator (Aeschylus); address of publisher (*Allan Kaprow*); maps (Allen, Katharine M., *American Junior Colleges*, Amerine, Anderson, Arbingast); contents of the book (Aeschylus); date of copyright, indicated by a *c* before the date, (Amerine, Anderson); and editor (*American Junior Colleges*).

By Author, Subject, and Title

A book that is listed in the Weekly Record of *Publishers' Weekly*, therefore is carefully described and identified, but it is listed only under the name of its author. The next step, to make it available also by its title and by its subject, is accomplished by *American Book Publishing Record*,[7] a monthly cumulation of items from the Weekly Record arranged, as if on the shelves of a library, by the Dewey Decimal Classification (Figure 5). This classified list is accompanied by an index of authors and also by an index of titles and subjects. Thus, at least in theory, within a week after publication it is possible to find a description of a book under the name of its author, and within a month to find it listed by author, title, and subject. In practice, however, it cannot be assumed that the timing will work out quite so neatly.

At this point the new book may also appear in another monthly trade bibliography, the *Cumulative Book Index*,[8] issued by the H.W. Wilson Company. A page from this publication (Figure 6) shows several variations from the lists previously mentioned. The *CBI*, as it is often called, includes in one alphabet the names of authors (Laing, Laklan, Lambert), titles (*The lame dog man, The landscape of Australian poetry*), and subjects (Land tenure, Landlord and tenant, Language and languages) of the books

---

[7]*American Book Publishing Record* (New York: R.R. Bowker Company, 1960-date), monthly with annual cumulations.
[8]*Cumulative Book Index* (New York: The H.W. Wilson Co., 1898–date), monthly with cumulations.

AMERICAN BOOK PUBLISHING RECORD

The basic arrangement in the following pages is by Dewey Decimal Classification with separate sections appended for juvenile books, fiction, and talking books (phonorecords) which could not more logically be classified by subject. Separate author and title indexes are included at the end of the text. Included in the title index are many important divisions within the Dewey Decimal Classification which may be of interest to particular readers.

Main divisions of the Dewey Decimal Classification are given below; these categories are repeated above each page to which they apply, along with the actual range of numbers used on that page. Also included below are some examples of important divisions within the Dewey Decimal Classification.

000 **General Works**	400 **Language**	700 **The Arts**
100 **Philosophy**	500 **Pure Science**	780 Music
200 **Religion**	600 **Technology**	790 Sports
300 **Social Science**	610 Medicine	800 **Literature**
330 Economics	620 Engineering	900 **History**
340 Law	630 Agriculture	910 Travel
370 Education	650 Business	920 Biography

000 GENERAL WORKS

AMOSOV, Nikolai Mikhailovich 001.5'35
Modeling of thinking and the mind [by] N. M. Amosov. Tr. by Leo Finegold. Tr. ed.: Lawrence J. Fogel. New York, Spartan [1967] xiii, 192p. illus. 25cm. Tr. of (romanized: Modelirovanie myshieniia i psikhiki) [Q335.A4513 1967] 67-27007 12.00
1. Artificial intelligence. I. Title.
For cyberneticists, psychologists and computer scientists interested in simulation problems.

†WILLIAMS, Raymond 001.55
Communications. Rev. ed. New York, Barnes & Noble [1967] 196p. tables. 22½cm. First pub. by Chatto & Windus, London, 1962. [P92.G7W5 1966] 67-70095 5.75
1. Communication—Gt. Brit. I. Title.

LORENZEN, Coral E., 1925- 001'.9
Flying saucer occupants [by] Coral and Jim Lorenzen. Introd. by Frank B. Salisbury. [New York] New Amer. Lib. [1967] 215p. illus. 18cm. (A Signet bk. T3205) A selection of reports about unidentified flying objects seen on the ground, and their occupants, from the Aerial Phenomena Research Organization (APRO) Bibl. [TL 789.L59] 67-8277 pap., .75
1. Flying saucers. I. Lorenzen, Jim, joint author. II. Aerial Phenomena Research Organization. III. Title.

†PUBLISHERS' *trade list annual* 015.73
(*The*); 95th 196?-New York, Bowker, 1967.

1953-1957, H. B. Anstaett; 1958- S. L. Prakken [Z1215.P972]
SUBJECT guide to Books in print; an index to the Publisher's trade list annual. 1967. New York, Bowker, 1967. v. 29-cm. annual. Eds.: 1957. H. B. Anstaett, S. L. Prakken; 1958- S. L. Prakken [Z1215. P973] 4-12648rev3* See note below for prices
1. Catalogs, Publishers'—U. S. 2. American literature—Bibl. 3. English literature—Bibl. I. Leypoldt Frederick, 1835-1884. II. Uhlendorf, Bernhard Alexander, 1893- ed. III. Anstaett, Herbert Bulow, 1902- ed. IV. Prakken, Sarah L., ed. V. Bowker (R.R.) Company, firm, publishers, New York. VI. Title: Books in print. VII. Title: Subject guide to Books in print.
Publishers' Trade List Annual, set $14.00; Books in Print, set, $19.85; Subject Guide to Books in Print, set, $18.25.

WHITE, Alex Sandri 016.016
Fact-finding made easy; a new guide to informational sources, by A. Sandir White. New, updated ed. Allenhurst, N.J., Aurea Pubns. [1967] 129 1. 30cm. [Z1002.W45 1967] 67-3292 5.40
1. Bibliography—Bibl. 2. Reference books —Bibl. 3. Information services—U.S. I. Title.

PERKINS, Ralph 016.028
Book selection media; a descriptive guide to 170 aids for selecting library materials. Rev. Champaign, Ill., Natl. Council of Teachers of English, 1967. xxiii, 168p. 22cm. [Z1035. A1P37 1967] 67-8286 pap., 2.00
1. Book selection. 2. Bibliography—Bibl. I. National Council of Teachers of English. II. Title.

WINCKLER, Paul A 016.21

FIGURE 5. AMERICAN BOOK PUBLISHING RECORD [*American Book Publishing Record* (R. R. Bowker Company). Used by permission of the publisher.]

Lagomorpha, Fossil
Dawson, M. R. Oreolagus and other lagomorpha (mammalia) from the miocene of Colorado, Wyoming, and Oregon. pa $1 '65 Univ. of Colo. press
Laidlaw-Dickson, Donald James
(ed) See Aeromodeller (periodical). Annual
Laing, Alexander Kinnan, 1903-
(ed) See Laing, D. B. The collected poems of Dilys Laing
Laing, Mrs Alexander Kinnan. See Laing, D. B.
Laing, Dilys (Bennett) (Mrs Alexander Kinnan Laing) 1906-1960
The collected poems of Dilys Laing; with an introd. by M. L. Rosenthal [ed. by Alexander Laing] xxxi,464p $8.50 '67 Western reserve univ. press   LC 67-14519
Laite, Gordon
(il) See Mahābhārata. The five sons of King Pandu
Laklan, Carli (Mrs James Arello)
Surf with me. 160p $3.95 '67 McGraw
                                    LC 67-24956
Lamb, Charles, 1775-1834
Blunden, E. C. Charles Lamb and his contemporaries. $6 '67 Shoe String
Lamb, John William
The Archbishopric of York: the early years; with a foreword by the Archbishop of York. 156p pa 12s 6d '67 Faith press
Lambert, Elisabeth (Mrs Cesar Ortiz)
The complete book of Mexican cooking; drawings by Roger Chapin. 352p $7.95 '67 Evans, M.&co.   LC 67-18534
The lame dog man. Turner, G. R. Aus$3.75 Cassell
L'Amour, Louis, 1908-
Hondo. 158p 10s 6d '67 Jenkins
Lampe, Geoffrey William Hugo, 1912-
The seal of the Spirit; a study in the doctrine of baptism and confirmation in the New Testament and the Fathers; 2d ed. with corrections. a new introd. and add. bibliography. xxvii,344p 35s '67 S.P.C.K.
Lamport, Felicia, 1916-
Cultural slag; drawings by Edward Gorey. 136p $3.95 '66 Houghton; 21s '67 Gollancz
Landscape   LC 66-19839;67-107947(GB)
Shepard, P. Man in the landscape. $6.95 '67 Knopf
The landscape of Australian poetry. Elliott, B. R. Aus$7.50 Cheshire, F.W.
          univ. press

Lang, Maria, pseud. See Lange, D.
Lange, Dagmar
Death awaits thee, by Maria Lang [pseud] tr. by Joan Tate. 189p 18s '67 Hodder
Lange, Victor, 1908-
Modern German literature, 1870-1940. 223p $7 '67 Kennikat   LC 67-27616
Langer, Susanne Katherina (Knauth) 1895-
An introduction to symbolic logic. 3d rev ed 367p pa $1.85 '67 Dover   LC 66-29834
Langley, Harold David, 1925-
Social reform in the United States navy, 1798-1862. 309p $8.50 (64s) '67 Univ. of Ill. press   LC 67-10440
Langton, John William
Sheet metal production; ed. by A. H. Garvey. 191p il 35s '67 Pitman
Language, Universal
Ogden, C. K. Opposition. $3.50; pa $1.50 (pa 12s) '67 Ind. univ. press
Language and languages
Fraenkel, G. Language in culture. pa $1.32 '67 Ginn
Fraenkel, G. Languages of the world. pa $1.88 '67 Ginn
Hevesi, J. L. ed. Essays on language and literature. $7 '67 Kennikat
Richards, I. A. Speculative instruments. pa $1.95 '67 Harcourt
Language and mental retardation. Schiefelbusch, R. L. and others, eds. $5.95 Holt
Language in uniform. Ford, N. A. comp. pa $1.45 Odyssey
The language of chemistry. Walker, R. A. and Johnston, H. pa $2.95 Prentice-Hall
Language of fiction. 3d ptg Lodge, D. pa $2.95 (pa 21s) Columbia univ. press
The language of painting. Barron, J. N. $4.95 World pub.
Languages

            Psychology
Jakobovits, L. A. and Miron, M. S. eds. Readings in the psychology of language. $9.95 '67 Prentice-Hall
Schiefelbusch, R. L. and others, eds. Language and mental retardation. $5.95 '67 Holt
Languages, Modern

            Study and teaching
Donoghue, M. R. comp. Foreign languages and the schools. pa $4.95 '67 Brown, W.C.
Stern, H. H. Foreign languages in primary education. new   Oxford

listed. There are cross references from the names of editors (Laing, Alexander Kinnan), joint authors (Lape, Elizabeth Baymore), and pseudonyms (Lang, Maria). It is only in the author entry, however, that full bibliographic information may be found, such as the number of pages or the author's full name. Prices for some of the books are given in foreign currencies (Lane, Carl Daniel; Lascaris, Constantino) indicating that these books were published outside the United States. The *CBI* does, in fact, try to list all publications written in the English language, wherever they may be published.

The National Union Catalog
As A Current National Bibliography

A book published in the United States is almost certain to be acquired by the Library of Congress, usually through the deposit of copies required for copyright. When it is cataloged by this library it is also listed in a monthly issue of the *National Union Catalog*,[9] a publication which plays a dual role in American bibliography. As a union catalog it will be described in a later chapter. As a current national bibliography it performs an important function by listing the books received and cataloged by the Library of Congress and additional titles received and cataloged by some 750 North American libraries, thus encompassing almost all the books published in the United States. It is arranged by author (Figure 7), and its entries, printed from type prepared for catalog cards, contain much the same bibliographic information as those in the Weekly Record section of *Publishers' Weekly*. Additional symbols, shown in the lower left-hand corner of some of the cards, pertain to the union catalog function and may be ignored for the present.

The page from the *National Union Catalog* in Figure 7, from the issue for October 1967, shows, among a number of foreign titles, some which were published in the United States in 1965, 1966, and 1967. (Brickman, Morrie; Brewster, Dorothy; Brewster, Adolph). The monthly issues are restricted to works published during the current year and the two preceding years, although the cumulated volumes (quarterly, annual, quinquennial) include all the books cataloged during the period covered, regardless of their dates of publication. It is interesting to note that certain classes of publications that are of marginal commercial interest and are largely excluded from the Bowker and Wilson lists are represented here: theses (Brictson, Bridge, Bridgeman), government publications (Bricker),

---

[9]*National Union Catalog: A Cumulative Author List Representing Library of Congress Printed Cards, and Titles Reported by Other American Libraries* (Washington: Library of Congress, 1956–date), monthly with cumulations.

The National Union Catalog

Brewster, Adolph Brewster, 1854–1937.
The hill tribes of Fiji; a record of forty years' intimate
connection with the tribes ... New York, Johnson Reprint
Corp. [1967]
308 p. illus., fold. map. 22 cm. (Landmarks in anthropology)
Title page includes original imprint: Philadelphia, Lippincott,
1922.
1. Fijians. 2. Fiji Islands—Soc. life & cust. I. Title.
DU600.B7 1967 390'.0996'11 67-8674

Brewster, Dorothy, 1883–
Aaron Hill, poet, dramatist, projector.
New York, AMS Press, 1966.
300 p.
1. Hill, Aaron, 1685–1750.
KMK NUC67-84984

Brewton, John Edmund, 1898–
Books about books for children and youth.
A classified bibliography. Compiled by
John E. Brewton and Frances Walsh. Nash-
ville, Tenn., Dept. of English, George
Peabody College for Teachers, 1965.
34 l. 28 cm.
TNJ-P NUC67-84774

Brezetz, André Betge-
see Betge-Brezetz, André.

Březina, Otakar
see Jebavý, Václav, 1869–1929.

Briandt, Calle, 1919–
Alpin skidåkning [av] Calle Briandt [och]
Sigge Wall. [Halmstad] Wahlström &
Widstrand [1966–
v. illus. 19 cm. (Den Moderna Hand-
boken)
1. Skis and skiing. I. Wall, Sigge, joint
author. II. Title.
OU NUC67-85309

Bricaud, Jean.
L'administration du département d'Ille-et-
Vilaine au début de la révolution, 1790–1791.
Rennes, Impr. Bretonne, 1965.
572 p. (Travaux de la Société d'histoire du
droit et des institutions des pays de l'ouest
de la France, v. 3)
Includes bibliography.
1. Ille-et-Vilaine, France (Dept.)—Hist.—
Revolution, 1790–1792. I. Title. (Series:
Société d'histoire du droit et des institutions
des pays de l'ouest de la France. Travaux,
v. 3)
ICU IU NUC67-84847

Brice, William Charles
see Fitzgerald, Walter, 1898–1949. Africa...
10th ed. revised. London, Methuen, 1967.

Briceño Werner, Sergio.
24 [i.e. Veinticuatro] horas en la ciudad.
2. ed. Santiago de Chile, Editorial Orbe
[1965]
125 p. 19 cm.
I. Title.
TxU NUC67-84645

Bricker, Neal S.
Solute and water transport across biologic
membranes. Washington, U.S. Govt. Print.
Off. , 1966.
28 p. (U.S. Office of Saline Water.
Research and development progress report
no. 206)
DNAL NUC67-85357

Brickhill, Paul.
The Dam Busters. With a foreword by
Lord Tedder. [1st American ed.] New York,
Ballantine Books [1965, c1951]
185 p. 19 cm.
1. Gt. Brit. Royal Air Force. 617 Squadron.
2. World War, 1939–1945–Aerial operations,
British. I. Title.
NBuU NUC67-85799

Brickhill, Paul.
La grande évasion. Texte français de
R. Jouan. Illustrations de François Batet.
[Paris] Hachette [c1965]
248 p. illus. 17 cm. (Bibliothèque verte,
271)
1. World War, 1939–1945–Prisoners &
prisons. German. 2. World War, 1939–1945–
Personal narratives, English. 3. Escapes.
I. Title.
NB NUC67-85128

Brickman, Morrie.
This little Pigeon went to market; a saga of
man's search for a fraction. Chicago, Rand
McNally [1965]
1 v. (mostly illus.) 13 x 20 cm.
1. Investments–Caricatures and cartoons.
2. Capitalists and financiers–Caricatures and
cartoons. I. Title.
CoU NUC67-85373

Brickmann, A.
see Cairo, Nilo. Guia de medicina homeo-
pática. 20. ed. , rev. São Paulo, Livraria
Teixeira, 1967.

Brictson, Clyde Alan.
Measures of pilot performance: comparative
analysis of day and night carrier recoveries.
[n. p.] 1966.
viii, 137 l. illus. 28 cm.
Thesis—Univ. of Southern California.
Typewritten.
1. Air pilots. 2. Aeroplane carriers.
I. Title.
CLSU NUC67-85958

Brīdaka, Lija.
Zem pērkona debesīm; dzejoļi. Rīgā,
Liesma, 1966.
106 p. front.
Russian title from colophon: Pod grozovymi
nebesami; stikhi.
MH DLC IU NUC67-84700

Bridge, John Leslie, 1939–
Aggregate excess demand, spare capacity
and the foreign trade of the United Kingdom,
1954–64. [Ithaca, N.Y.] 1966.
vii, 130 l. illus. 29 cm.
Thesis (Ph.D.)–Cornell University.
1. Gt. Brit.–Comm.–Mathematical models.
2. Gt. Brit.–Economic policy–Mathematical
models. I. Title.
NIC NUC67-84833

Bridgeman, Loraine I.
Oral paragraphs in Kaiwa (Guarani)
[Bloomington, Ind.] 1966.
151 p.
Thesis (Ph. D.)–Indiana University.
Vita.
InU NUC67-84564

Bridges, Donald Wayne, joint author
see Churchward, Philip E. Tungsten
recovery from low-grade concentrates...
[Washington] U. S. Dept. of the Interior,
Bureau of Mines [1966]

FIGURE 7. NATIONAL UNION CATALOG

and very small pamphlets such as Frank W. Bridges' *A Brief History of the Theatre at Austin Junior College*, which consists of only fourteen leaves.[10] On the other hand, certain materials which are not usually cataloged by the Library of Congress, such as juvenile texts, paperback reprints, or jokebooks, are missing. The *National Union Catalog* is considered the most comprehensive current bibliography of books published in the United States;[11] but it is only through a combination of *Publishers' Weekly*, the *American Book Publishing Record*, the *Cumulative Book Index*, and the *National Union Catalog* that the approximately 30,000 new books issued each year in the United States receive, on the whole, adequate bibliographic coverage.

FOREIGN CURRENT NATIONAL AND TRADE BIBLIOGRAPHY

The United States would seem to have done as well as most nations and better than some in solving the problems of the orderly presentation of its currently published records. A recent study has shown that of eighty-seven nations surveyed, twenty-four possessed no bibliography that could properly be called a current national or trade bibliography.[12] The others had bibliographies which ranged from a relatively primitive list to a comprehensive and sophisticated system. From its earliest beginnings the United Nations Educational, Scientific, and Cultural Organization has advocated and encouraged the development of adequate national bibliographies. Its efforts have met with success, particularly among the developing nations. Much, however, remains to be done before the books of the world, particularly those currently being published, are adequately accounted for.

SUGGESTIONS FOR FURTHER INVESTIGATION

I. Is there a current national or trade bibliography for a country in which you are interested? If so, identify it. What kinds of publications does it include? What kinds does it exclude? If there is none, what lists might be used as partial substitutes for a current national or trade bibliography?

II. *Bibliografía de Centroamérica y del Caribe*, 1956–date (Havana-

---

[10]A leaf consists of one sheet of paper which may be printed on both sides to form two pages. Often it is printed on one side only.

[11]Roger C. Greer, "National Bibliography," *Library Trends*, XV, No. 3 (1967), 370.

[12]*Ibid.*, p. 362.

Madrid: Agrupación Bibliográfica Cubana José Toribio Medina, 1958–date) is a regional current bibliography including books published in Costa Rica, Cuba, El Salvador, Guatemala, Haiti, Honduras, Nicaragua, Panama, Puerto Rico, and the Dominican Republic. Are there other regional current bibliographies? If so, identify one.

III. Theses and dissertations are often excluded from current national or trade bibliographies. Can you identify a current bibliography for theses or dissertations in the United States?

IV. Identify one or more of the following and assess its usefulness to you:
   A. a catalog of books currently in print in the United States
   B. a catalog of books currently in print in a foreign country
   C. a current list of pamphlets published in the United States

References for the preceding problems

Collison, Robert L., *Bibliographical Services Throughout the World, 1950–1959*. Paris: United Nations Educational, Scientific, and Cultural Organization, 1961. Later developments are noted in the bimonthly issues of *Bibliography, Documentation, Terminology*, 1961–date (Paris: United Nations Educational, Scientific, and Cultural Organization, 1961–date).

Greer, Roger C., "National Bibliography," *Library Trends*, XV, No. 3 (1967), 350–77.

Malclès, Louise-Noëlle, *Les Sources du Travail Bibliographique*. Genève: E. Droz; Lille: Giard, 1950–58, 4 vols.

Winchell, Constance M., *Guide to Reference Books*. 8th ed. Chicago: American Library Association, 1967; *First Supplement, 1965–1966*. Chicago: American Library Association, 1968.

III

RETROSPECTIVE NATIONAL
AND TRADE BIBLIOGRAPHY

*A painfull work it is I'll assure you, and more than
difficult, wherein what toyle hath been taken, as no
man thinketh so no man believeth, but he hath
made the triall.*

—*Anthony à Wood*[1]

What books were available to Cotton Mather's audiences? When was
Hawthorne's popularity at its peak? What biographies of Lincoln appeared
during the campaign of 1860? Such questions can most readily be answered
by consulting a reliable record of the publications of past years within the
United States, in other words, by referring to the retrospective bibliography
of that country. Unfortunately, retrospective bibliography is likely to be
uneven or, possibly, non-existent until the date at which a country first
developed a comprehensive current national or trade bibliography. In
Germany this watershed year is 1812, in France, 1827, in Great Britain,
1835. During the centennial year 1876, which saw a flowering of American
librarianship, the *American Catalogue of Books in Print and For Sale*, the
first comprehensive trade bibliography in the United States, was published.
Earlier periods in this country are covered by an assortment of lists which
vary as widely as the interests and temperaments of the men who produced them, and it is largely due to the labors of numerous scholars,
librarians, bibliographers, and booksellers that these early books have been
searched out and identified.

---

[1]Quoted by Joseph Sabin on the title page to his *Dictionary of Books Relating
to America.*

FOUR RETROSPECTIVE LISTS:
THE UNITED STATES

Four major lists, each covering a particular period, record with varying degrees of thoroughness the American books published from the introduction of the printing press into the colonies in 1639 to the beginning of comprehensive trade bibliography in 1876. A fifth list, spanning all of American history, but with many limitations, is usually included as part of American retrospective bibliography. Covering the earliest period is a list compiled by Charles Evans, a librarian who labored for more than thirty years on his *American Bibliography.*[1] Originally he had planned to include the years 1639 to 1820, but at the age of eighty-four he decided to make 1800 the terminal date for his bibliography. He died in 1935, before he had completed the year 1799 of his work, and it was twenty years before others had carried his list through 1800.[2] Believing that the date was the most important element in the description of these early books, Evans arranged his list first by the year of publication, and within each year by the author (or by the title, if the work was anonymous). The page from Evans' work reproduced in Figure 8 shows, for the year 1786, a newspaper and a periodical (numbers 19518 and 19519) and what appears to be a speech (number 19520), as well as a number of books. The titles, often very long (numbers 19520, 19521, 19522), are fully recorded. In addition, the number of pages[3] and the size of the volume[4] are given. The symbols near the right-hand margin (AAS, LOC, BA, *etc.*) indicate the libraries where copies of these works are located, and the column at the extreme right of the page records, when such information is available, the prices that these books have brought at auction. Two indexes to the thirteen volumes of Evans' work, one of authors and titles[5] and the other of printers,[6] com-

[1]Charles Evans, *American Bibliography: A Chronological Dictionary of All Books, Pamphlets and Periodical Publications Printed in the United States of America from the Genesis of Printing in 1639 down to and Including the Year 1800* (Chicago: Privately printed for the author at the Blakely Press, 1903–34), 12 vols.

[2]Clifford K. Shipton, *The American Bibliography of Charles Evans: A Chronological Dictionary of All Books, Pamphlets and Periodical Publications Printed in the United States of America from the Genesis of Printing in 1639 down to and Including the Year 1800* (Worcester, Mass.: American Antiquarian Society, 1955), vol. 13.

[3]A broadside (number 19521) is one sheet printed on one side.

[4]Indicated by *8vo* (octavo), *4to* (quarto), *fol.* (folio), etc.

[5]Roger P. Bristol, *The American Bibliography of Charles Evans: A Chronological Dictionary of All Books, Pamphlets and Periodical Publications Printed in the United States of America from the Genesis of Printing in 1639 down to and Including the Year 1800* (Worcester, Mass.: American Antiquarian Society, 1959), vol. 14, index.

[6]Roger P. Bristol, *Index of Printers, Publishers, and Booksellers Indicated by Charles Evans in His American Bibliography* (Charlottesville, Va.: Bibliographical Society of the University of Virginia, 1961).

19517   BOSTON. MASSACHUSETTS. KING'S CHAPEL.
         A CATECHISM, FOR THE INSTRUCTION OF CHILDREN ; TAKEN FROM THE LITURGY OF
         THE CHAPEL CHURCH IN BOSTON.
               Boston: Printed and sold by Peter Edes, in State-Street. 1786.

19518   THE BOSTON [cut] GAZETTE, AND THE COUNTRY JOURNAL. CONTAINING THE LATEST
         OCCURRENCES, FOREIGN AND DOMESTIC. [Motto.] No. 1643. MONDAY, JANUARY
         2, [— No. 1692. MONDAY, DECEMBER 25, 1786.]
               Printed by Benjamin Edes and Son, No. 42, *Cornhill, Boston.* 1786. fol.
         The motto reads: A free press maintains the majesty of the people.
         The cut represents Liberty freeing a bird from its cage, with the legend:
         Libertas et natale solum.

19519   THE BOSTON MAGAZINE FOR THE YEAR 1786. CONTAINING, A COLLECTION OF
         INSTRUCTIVE AND ENTERTAINING ESSAYS, IN THE VARIOUS BRANCHES OF USEFUL,
         AND POLITE LITERATURE. TOGETHER WITH FOREIGN AND DOMESTICK OCCUR-
         RENCES, ANECDOTES, OBSERVATIONS ON THE WEATHER, &C. &C. VOL. III. [JANU-
         ARY – OCTOBER, 1786.]
               *Boston: Printed and published by Edmund Freeman, north side of the
         [Town-Dock] State-House.* 1786. pp. (2), 451. 8vo.   AAS. LOC.
         Discontinued with the number for October, 1786.

19520   BOWDOIN, JAMES   1727 – 1790
         A PHILOSOPHICAL DISCOURSE TO THE AMERICAN ACADEMY OF ARTS AND SCIENCES ;
         TO WHICH ARE ADDED THREE MEMOIRS ON PHILOSOPHICAL SUBJECTS. THE WHOLE
         EXTRACTED FROM THE FIRST VOLUME OF THE MEMOIRS OF THE ACADEMY LATELY
         PUBLISHED. BY JAMES BOWDOIN, ESQUIRE, . . .
               Boston: Printed by Adams and Nourse. M.DCC.LXXXVI. pp. 71,
         plate. 4to.   BA.

19521   BOWEN, JABEZ   1739 – 1815
         TO THE FREEMEN OF THE STATE OF RHODE-ISLAND, &C. GENTLEMEN, WELL CON-
         VINCED THAT THE SUPPORTERS OF THE PRESENT OPPOSITION . . . HAVE CIRCU-
         LATED, . . . THAT THE INTEREST ON THE STATE AND CONTINENTAL SECURITIES
         HAVE BEEN PAID ON THE NOMINAL SUMS, AND NOT ON THE REAL VALUE; I HAVE
         PROCURED A CERTIFICATE FROM YOUR GENERAL-TREASURER, [which is added.]
               [Providence: Printed by John Carter, 1786.] Broadside. fol.   JCB. LOC.

19522   BOWLER, METCALF   – 1789
         A TREATISE ON AGRICULTURE AND PRACTICAL HUSBANDRY. DESIGNED FOR THE
         INFORMATION OF LAND-OWNERS AND FARMERS. WITH A BRIEF ACCOUNT OF THE
         ADVANTAGES ARISING FROM THE NEW METHOD OF CULTURE, AS NOW PRACTISED
         IN EUROPE. [Twelve lines of quotations.] BY METCALF BOWLER, ESQ.
               Providence: Printed by Bennett Wheeler, for the Author, 1786. pp. [88.] 8vo.

19523   BROOK, MARY BROTHERTON   1726 – 1782
         GRÜNDE FÜR DIE NOTHWENDIGKEIT EINES STILLEN HARRENS BEYM OEFFENT-
         LICHEN GOTTESDIENST, . . .
               Philadelphia: Gedruckt bey Carl Cist, 1786. pp. 38. 8vo.   BM.

19524   THE BROTHER'S GIFT: OR, THE NAUGHTY GIRL REFORMED. [Four lines of verse.]
         THE FIRST WORCESTER EDITION.
               Worcester, Massachusetts Printed by Isaiah Thomas . . . MDCCLXXXVI.
         pp. 30. 32mo.   AAS.

FIGURE 8.   EVANS' AMERICAN BIBLIOGRAPHY, 1639–1800

plete the set. Evans loved these unpretentious, often crudely printed early books and the sober, earnest folk who produced them. He personally examined every copy he could find, and his work is surprisingly free from errors.

The years from 1800 to 1820, which Evans had planned to cover, remained for many years a bibliographic no-man's-land. Finally, in 1958, there began to appear a series of volumes compiled by Ralph Shaw and Richard Shoemaker which cover the bibliography of this period.[7] In general the Shaw and Shoemaker volumes follow the methods used by Evans and, like the older bibliography, give the location of copies of the books listed (Figure 9). However, they were less carefully compiled than was Evans' bibliography. On the page shown in Figure 9, for example, entry number 968 lacks the author's first name, gives only the briefest of titles, and omits the name of the publisher as well as the number of pages and size of the volume. Hampered by lack of time and funds, the compilers were unable to examine personally all the works listed and were forced to rely heavily on descriptions in secondary sources. Errors were inevitable, and the lists should be used with caution. Under the title *Early American Imprints*[8] the works recorded by Evans have been collected in a microprint edition where they are arranged by the numbers which Evans assigned to them. A similar collection is being made of the items included by Shaw and Shoemaker.[9]

The period from 1820 to 1861 is covered by a third bibliography, compiled by Orville Roorbach,[10] a bookseller whose work was intended not so much for scholars as for his fellow booksellers (Figure 10). He arranged his books by title as well as by author (see entries for *The Linwoods, Lissie Lindon*, and others), but the description he gives is scanty. Authors' names are often incomplete (see entry for *Lionel Lincoln*), and dates of publication and number of pages are omitted. Incomplete and often inaccurate as it is, however, Roorbach's is the only general bibliography for its period. Another bibliography has recently been undertaken to give coverage to these years.[11] When completed, it is expected to include far more titles than does Roorbach.

---

[7]Ralph R. Shaw and Richard H. Shoemaker, *American Bibliography: A Preliminary Checklist, 1801–1819* (New York: The Scarecrow Press, Inc., 1958–1966), 22 vols.

[8]*Early American Imprints, 1639–1800* (Worcester, Mass.: American Antiquarian Society, 1956).

[9]*Ibid.*, second series, 1801–1819 (Worcester, Mass.: American Antiquarian Society, 1964–   ), in progress.

[10]Orville A. Roorbach, *Bibliotheca Americana, 1820–1861* (New York: Orville A. Roorbach, 1852–61), 4 vols.

[11]Richard H. Shoemaker, *Checklist of American Imprints, 1820–*   (New York: The Scarecrow Press, Inc., 1964–   ), in progress.

Morton, Thomas
    Speed the plough... 2d Amer. ed. Philadelphia, pub.
by John Conrad, & Co... Michael and John Conrad, &
Co... Baltimore - & Rapin, Conrad, & Co., Washington
City, 1801. 96p. MWA.   963

A Mournful Tragedy. Giving an account of the shocking
and unprecedented Catastrophe, which happened at Dedham
the 18th day of May, 1801, between Mr. Jason Fairbanks,
aged 21, and Miss Eliza Fales, of 19... [1801?]. Broadside. MHi; MWA.   964

Muhlenberg, Henry
    Observations on the genera Juglans, Fraxinus, and
Quercus... [1801?]. 259p. DLC.   965

Mumford, Paul
    An oration, spoken in the Second Baptist meeting-
house, at Newport, on the Fourth of July, 1801... Newport, R.I., Pr. by Oliver Farnsworth, 1801. 23p. DLC;
MWA; NN; RP.   966

-- -- [2d. ed.]. Newport, R.I., Pr. by Oliver Farnsworth, 1801. MWA.   967

Munshall, J.
    Rural felicity... New York, 1801. MB.   968

Murray, John
    Jerubbaal, or tyranny's grove destroyed... Newbury-
port, Mass., Pr. by Edmund M. Blunt, 1801. 70p.
DLC; MBAt; MiD-B; MWA.   969

Murray, Lindley, 1745-1826.
    English exercises adapted to the grammar lately pub.
by L. Murray... Ed. 4 corrected. New York, 1801.
192p. NSyU; OCHP.   970

-- The English reader...3d Phila. ed. Philadelphia, Pr.
by B. & J. Johnson, 1801. 392p. NN.   971

-- Introduction to the English reader; or, A selection of
pieces, in prose and poetry; calculated to improve the

FIGURE 9. SHAW AND SHOEMAKER'S AMERICAN BIBLIOGRAPHY FOR
1801–1819 [Ralph R. Shaw and Richard H. Shoemaker, *American
Bibliography: A Preliminary Checklist* (New York: The Scarecrow
Press, 1958). Used by permission of the authors.]

Linn, W., The Legal and Commercial Common-Place Book.
8vo. law shp. . . . . 1 75 *Andrus, G. & Co.*
Linnard, Anna Jane, Memoir of. By Rev. Robt. Baird. cl. 0 42 *Whipple & Co.*
Linsley, Rev. J. H., Memoirs of. By his Daughter. 18mo. 0 38 *Robbins & S.*
Linwoods, The. By Miss Sedgwick. 2 v. . . . 1 50 *Harper & Bros.*
Lionel Lincoln. By Cooper. 2 v. pap. . . . . 0 50 *Stringer & T.*
Lippard, G., Bel of Prairie Eden. pap. . . . . 0 25 *T. B. Peterson.*
———— ———— Blanche of Brandywine. pap. . . . 0 75 "
———— ———— Legends of Mexico. pap. . . . 0 25 "
———— ———— " the Revolution. cl. . . . 1 50 *G. B. Zieber.* '47
———— ———— Mysteries and Miseries of Philadelphia. 2 pts. 1 00 *T. B. Peterson.*
———— ———— Paul Ardenheim, the Monk of Wissahikon. 2
parts, pap. . . . . . . 1 00 "
———— ———— The Empire City; or, New York by Night
and by Day. pap. . . . . 0 50 *Stringer & T.*
———— ———— The Nazarene; or, the last of the Washing-
tons. 2 parts, pap. . . . . . 1 00 *T. B. Peterson.*
———— ———— The Quaker City; or, the Monks of Monk
Hall. 2 parts, pap. . . . . 1 00 "
———— ———— Washington and his Generals; or, Legends of
the Revolution. 2 parts, pap. . . . . 1 00 "
Lipscomb, A. A., Social Spirit of Christianity. 8vo. cl. . *H. D. Moore.*
Lisco, F. G., The Parables of Jesus, Explained and Illus-
trated. Translated from the German by Rev. P. Fair-
bairn. 12mo. cl. . . . . 0 88 *Daniels & S.* '50
Lisfranc, M., Clinical Surgery. Translated by A. S. Doane.
8vo. . . . . *New York.* '45
———— ———— Diseases of the Uterus. Translated by G. H.
Lodge. 8vo. cl. . . . . . . 1 75 *Ticknor & Co.* '46
Lissie Linden. By Mrs. Hughs. sqr. cl. . . . 0 33 *Lindsay & B.* '49
List, C., Outlines of Astronomy. 18mo. hf. r. . . 0 31 *Thomas, C. & Co.* '46
———— ———— " Botany. 18mo. hf. r. . . 0 31 "
———— ———— " Natural Philosophy. 18mo. hf. r. . 0 31 " '46
Listener, The. By Caroline Fry. 2 v. cl. . . . 1 00 *Carter & Bros.*
Liston, Robert, Elements of Surgery. Edited by S. D.
Gross. shp. . . . . . . 3 00 *Barrington & H.*
———— ———— Lectures on the Operations of Surgery. With
Additions by T. D. Mutter. 8vo. shp. . 3 00 *Lea & B.* '46
———— ———— Practical Surgery. Notes, &c., by Norris. 8vo. 3 75 *Thomas, C. & Co.*
Literary Gem: an Illustrated Souvenir for all Seasons. . *G. S. Appleton.* '49
———— Portraits. *See Gilfillan, G.*
———— Reader, for High Schools and Academies. By Miss
A. Hall. 12mo. r. cl. sds. . . . 0 94 *J.P.Jewett & Co.* '50
———— and Scientific Class-Book. By L. W. Leonard. shp. 0 50 *J. & J.W. Prentiss*
Literature of American Local History. By H. E. Ludwig.
8vo. pap. . . . . *Author, N. Y.* '46
———— of Europe. *See Hallam, H.*
———— of the Age of Elizabeth. By Hazlitt. cl. . 0 50 *J. Wiley.*
———— (The), and The Literary Men of Great Britain and
Ireland. By A. Mills. 2 v. 8vo. cl. . . . 3 50 *Harper & Bros.* '51

FIGURE 10. ROORBACH'S BIBLIOTHECA AMERICANA, 1820–1861

Continuing the Roorbach list is the *American Catalogue*,[12] which James Kelly, a young Irishman, managed to bring out in spite of the devastating effects of the Civil War. Considering the difficulties under which he worked, it is not surprising that his work is full of inaccuracies. For example, the Washington Irving item in Figure 11 appears in one place in his catalog as *The Adventures of Captain Brownville*, in another as *Adventures of Captain Bonneville* (the correct title). Kelly intended his work to be a continuation of Roorbach's, but because of its many inaccuracies he was denied permission to designate it as such. Nevertheless, it forms the best available record for the publications of these very important years.

COMPREHENSIVE TRADE BIBLIOGRAPHY: ITS BEGINNINGS IN THE U.S.

With the appearance of *The American Catalogue of Books in Print and For Sale, July 1, 1876*[13] (not to be confused with Kelly's *American Catalogue*), the United States acquired its first comprehensive trade bibliography (Figure 12). The first volume of this work lists both authors and titles of the books. A second volume serves as a subject list. Supplementary volumes followed at more or less regular intervals until 1910, when *The American Catalogue of Books in Print and for Sale* was succeeded by its rival, the *United States Catalog*,[14] which the H.W. Wilson Company had been publishing since 1898. This catalog of books in print and for sale (Figure 13) was supplemented by the *Cumulative Book Index*, issued periodically with cumulations. When the *United States Catalog* ceased publication in 1928, it was succeeded by the permanent cumulations of the *CBI*. The monthly issues continue to list new books as they appear.

AN AMBITIOUS BIBLIOGRAPHY

Spanning the field of American history, but with continually diminishing completeness, is the twenty-nine volume bibliography begun in 1868 by Joseph Sabin and requiring the work of many others to complete.[15] Sabin

---

[12]James Kelly, *American Catalogue of Books, Original and Reprints, Published in the United States from Jan., 1861, to Jan., 1871, With Date of Publication, Size, Price, and Publisher's Name* (New York: John Wiley & Sons, Inc., 1866–71), 2 vols.

[13]*The American Catalogue of Books in Print and for Sale, July 1, 1876* (New York: Publishers' Weekly, 1876), 2 vols.

[14]*United States Catalog: Books in Print, 1899–1928* (New York: The H.W. Wilson Company, 1900–1928), 4 vols.

[15]Joseph Sabin, *Dictionary of Books Relating to America, From Its Discovery to the Present Time* (New York: Sabin, 1868–92; Bibliographical Society of America, 1928–36). 29 vols.

Addy, D. C. (D.D.), Walter's Tour in the East. 6 vols., 16mo. cl., per vol., 90 cts. N. Y. .... *Sheldon & Co* 1864

Aden, Power; or, The Cost of a Scheme. By F. Owen. 8vo. pap., 75 cts. Boston. .... *Burnham* 1862

Adirondack (The); or, Life in the Woods. By J. T. Headley. New and enlarged ed., 12mo. plates, cl., $2 00. N. Y. .... *C. Scribner* 1864

Adjutant General's Report of the State of New York—1862-3-4. 4 vols. 8vo. cl. .... *Albany* 1862-4

Adlard, Geo., The Sutton-Dudleys of England and the Dudleys of Massachusetts, from the Roman Conquest to the Present Time. 8vo. cl., $2 00. N. Y. .... *C. B. Richardson.* 1862

Adventures and Misfortunes of a Saxon Schoolmaster. 18mo. pap., 15 cts. N. Y. .... *P. O'Shea.* 1864

—— of Captain Brownville (The). By Washington Irving. 12mo. cl., $1 75. N. Y. .... *G. P. Putnam* 1861

—— of a Hymn. 18mo. cl., 35 cts. Phila. .... *Am. S. S. U.* 1865

—— of Dick Onslow among the Red Skins. A Book for Boys. Edited by W. G. Kingston. 16mo. cl., $1 25. Boston. .... *Tilton & Co* 1863

—— of Gil Blas of Santillane (The). Translated from the French of Le Sage, by T. Smollett. New ed. revised. 3 vols. 16mo. cl., $5 25. Boston. .... *Little, Brown & Co.* 1864

—— of a Missionary; or, Rivers of Waters in a Dry Place. 16mo. cl., $1 25. N. Y. .... *Carlton & Porter.* . 1864

—— of Philip on His Way through the World (The). By W. M. Thackeray. 8vo. cl., $2 00. N. Y. .. .. *Harpers* 1862

—— of Rob Roy (The). By James Grant. 16mo cl., $1 50. Boston.... *Crosby & A* 1864

Advice to a Mother on the Management of her Offspring. By P. H. Chavasse. 6th ed. 12mo., 50 cts., N. Y. .... *Baillière Bros.* 1862

Æsop, Fables of, with Life of the Author. 16mo. cl., $2 00. N. Y. ...... *Hurd & Houghton.* 1865

Iron, N. C. The Two Guards. 12mo. pap., 10 cts. N. Y. .... *Beadle & Co* 1863

—— Furnace (The); or, Slavery and Secession. By Rev. J. H. Aughey. 12mo. cl., $1 25. Phila. .... *Martiens.* 1863

Irrlichter (Die). Ein Märchen von der Verfasser in der Prinzessin Ilse. 16mo. pap., 50 cts. Boston. .... *S. R. Urbino.* ... 1864

Irving, E. (Rev.) Life of. By Mrs. Oliphant. 8vo. cl., $3 50. N. Y. ... *Harpers* 1862

—— J. T. Attorney (The); or The Correspondence of John Quod. 12mo. cl., $1 50. N. Y. .... *R. M. De Witt.* ... 1861

—— " Harry Harson; or, The Benevolent Bachelor. 12mo. cl., $1 50. N. Y. .... "   1861

—— W. Adventures of Captain Bonneville. 12mo. cl., $2 50. N. Y. .. *G. P. Putnam.* ... 1861

—— " Alhambra (The). Author's Revised Ed., with Illustrations. 12mo. cl., $2 50. N. Y. .... "   1861

—— " Crayon Miscellany (The). Revised Ed. 16mo. vel. cl., $1 75. N. Y. (For G. P. Putnam.). .... *Hurd & Houghton.* 1865

—— " Chronicles of the Conquest of Granada. Author's Revised Ed. 12mo. cl., $2 50. N. Y. .... *G. P. Putnam* 1862

—— " History of New York. By Diedrich Knickerbocker. 16mo. vel. cl., $1 75. N. Y. .... "   1864

—— " Hudson Legends (The). Comprising the Legend of Sleepy Hollow and Rip Van Winkle. 4to. Illustrations. cl. ex., $4 50; mor., $8 00. N. Y. .... "   1863

—— " Legend of Sleepy Hollow, from "The Sketch Book" of. 4to. Illustrated. Fancy bds., $1 75. N. Y. .... "   1863

—— " Life and Voyages of Christopher Columbus (The). 3 vols. 12mo., per vol., $2 50. N. Y. .... "   1861

—— " Life of George Washington. 5 vols. 12mo. cl., per vol., $2 50. N.Y. "   1861-2

—— " Life and Letters of. By his Nephew, P. M. Irving. 4 vols. 12mo. cl., per vol., $2 50. N. Y. .... "   1861-3

FIGURE 11. KELLY'S AMERICAN CATALOGUE, 1861-1871

THE AMERICAN CATALOGUE

OF BOOKS IN PRINT AND FOR SALE, JULY 1, 1876.

AUTHORS AND TITLES.

A., A. Miriam's trial. ill. 18°. 50c.............*Pott.*

A., E. Bible class guide : lessons on the four Gospels in harmony. 18°. '60. bds., 40c....*Whittaker.*

A., F. C. Looking up. ill. 18°. 50c.............*Pott.*

A., F. S. (*pseud.*) *See* Flint, *Miss* S. A.

A., L. L. (*pseud.*) *See* Adams, *Mrs.* G. M.

A., S. F. Great success. 16°. '71. $1.50..*H. A. Young.*

A., S. M. How to study the Old Test., in a series of questions. 1st ser.: Genesis to Samuel. sq. 18°. '73. 40c.; 75c.; bds., 25c.........*Randolph.*

A B C-bok för minstabegynnare. 12°. bds., 10c. *Engberg.*

A B C Buch, u. Lese-Schreib- u. Denkübungen, od. erstes Buch. 16°. bds., 15c.............*Ludwig.*

A B C (Das) in Bildern u. Bibelsprüchen. [Germ. and Eng.] 12°. pap., 10c.............*Radde.*

A B C of life. Child, A. B. 25c.............*Colby.*

A B C of whist. W., J. R. 25c....*Scribner, W. & A.*

A B C- u. Bilderbuch. 12°. pap., 10c.; 15c....*Radde.*

A B C- u. Buchstabir-Büchlein. ill. 32°. '60. 10c. *Am. Tr.*

A B C- u. erstes Unterrichtsbuch f. Sonntagschulen. 16°. bds., 20c.............*Ev. Assoc.*

Abbey, R: *continued.*

— Divine assessment for the support of the ministry; ed. by T. O. Summers. 12°. '57. pap., 20c. *So. Meth.*

— Ecce ecclesia; showing the essential identity of the church in all ages. ('68.) 4th ed. 12°. '75. $1.75.............*So. Meth.*

— Ecclesiastical constitution : origin and character of the church of Christ and the Gospel ministry. ('56.) 2d ed. 12°. '60. $1.50......*So. Meth.*

— Strictures on church government; ed. by T. O. Summers. 12°. '60. pap., 10c....*So. Meth.*

— *See also* Yerger, —, Snedes, —, *and* Abbey, R.

Abbey; or, taking it easy. 18°. 45c.....*Am. S. S.*

Abbey of Innismoyle. Kennedy, G. 25c....*Peterson.*

Abbey of Ross. Burke, O. J. 50c.; 75c. ...*Sadlier.*

Abbot, Ezra. Bibliography of works rel. to nature, etc., of the soul. *See* Alger, W. R., Critical hist. of doct. of a future life.

— *See also* Hudson, C. F., Critical Gk. and Eng. concord. to New Test.; —Orme, W., Memoir of controversy resp. three heavenly witnesses; — Smith, W: Bible dictionary.

Abbot, Fs. E. *See* McQuaid, B. J., *and* Abbot, F. E.

Abbot, H: L. Siege artillery in the campaign against

FIGURE 12. THE AMERICAN CATALOGUE OF BOOKS IN PRINT AND FOR SALE, JULY 1, 1876

UNITED STATES CATALOG

AN AUTHOR, TITLE and SUBJECT INDEX

BOOKS IN PRINT 1902

A

A
apple pie. Greenaway; K., il. 75c. Warne.
was an apple pie. 25c; 50c. Dutton.

A1 code. *$7.50. Am. Code.

A B C
A B C. Gaskin, Mrs. A. $1. McClurg.
alphabet book. 50c. Dutton.
book. March, F. A. *20c. Ginn.
code. 4th ed. *$5. Am. Code.
code. 5th ed. *$7. Am. Code.
for temperance nurseries. Wright, Mrs. J. M. 25c. Nat. Temp.
guide to bee-keeping. Webster, W. B. 50c; pa. 25c. Henneberry.
guide to correct conduct. (Alhambra ser.) 50c; pa. 30c. '00. Henneberry Co.
guide to photography. Baldwin, T. S. 50c; pa. 30c. Henneberry.
guide to poultry keeping. 50c; pa. 30c. '00. Henneberry Co.
handbook. Phillips, D. H., comp. 75c.; $1; $1.25. Phillips & Co., 109 University Pl. N. Y.
manual of materia medica and therapeutics. Clark, G: H. $1. Boericke.
of agriculture. Coffin, G: M. $1.25. Judd.
of animals. 25c. Warne.
of banks and banking. Nelson, S. A. 50c. Dutton.
of Bible pictu ... 75c. Dutton.

A., F. S.
Ralph Foster. 25c. Hurst.
A 439: autobiography of a piano, by 25 musical scribes. $1.50. '00. Dutton.

A. K. H. B. See Boyd, A. K. H.

A. L. A. See American Library Assn.

A. L. O. E, pseud. See Tucker, C. M.

A., M.
Nance Oldfield: comedy. pa. 15c. Baker, W. H.

A., P. S.
Adhemar de Belcastel. 75c. Christian Press.
(tr.) French prisoner in Russia. 45c. Chr.Press.

A., V. P.
Military wrinkles. 25c. Scribner.
A. Ward's wax figger show. pa. 25c. Baker, W. H.

Aarbert. Marshall, W: $1.50. Amsterdam.

Aaron, Mrs. C. B., and others.
Dragon flies versus mosquitoes.$1.50.Appleton.

Aaron, Eugene Murray.
Butterfly hunting in Carribees. $2. Scribner.
Washington: federal city. 25c. Levytype.

Aaron in the wild woods. Harris, J. C. $2. Houghton.

Aarons, J. S.
Golden rules of gynecology. *40c. Pelton.

Abandoned. Van Fossen, L. B. $1.50. Neely.
Abandoned. ... me. Munro.

FIGURE 13.   UNITED STATES CATALOG

was an Oxford man who became a bookseller and an authority on rare books about America. His original plan was to include in his bibliography all works concerned with the political, governmental, military, social, and religious history of the entire Western Hemisphere, from its discovery until his day. Like Charles Evans he attempted more than he was able to accomplish in his lifetime. At his death he had completed thirteen volumes. The work was continued by Wilberforce Eames, librarian of the Lenox Library, who carried it through volume twenty by 1892. Nothing further was done until 1927, when a Carnegie grant made it possible to continue the work. It was finally completed in 1936 and published by the Bibliographical Society of America.

The page from Sabin's *Dictionary* in Figure 14 includes two German imprints (numbers 11656 and 11659), and two French (numbers [11658] and 11660), along with an American periodical (number [11661]) and some United States government publications (numbers 11662–11664), illustrating part of the range that Sabin originally planned for his list. With the passage of time, however, it became clear that if the work were to be completed its scope would have to be drastically reduced. After volume twenty, therefore, all titles published since 1876 were dropped. (These were being listed in the new trade bibliographies.) Broadsides printed after 1800 also were dropped. Futher restrictions followed: government publications were omitted, as were unimportant sermons, collections of world travel, general poetry, drama, and fiction after 1800 (unless of historical importance, in which case it was included until 1830), and so on. Perhaps no work illustrates better than Sabin's the patchwork type of retrospective national bibliography that is all too common as the result of overambitious planning and lack of time and funds.

FOREIGN RETROSPECTIVE BIBLIOGRAPHY

The chart in Figure 15 shows the outlines of American retrospective bibliography from the earliest period to the present. Until the year 1876 the work is chiefly that of amateur bibliographers, often with insufficient time and capital, and almost always inclined to underestimate the amount of each necessary to produce a first-rate bibliography. After 1876 the picture is clearer, with comprehensive trade bibliography supplying a more adequate bibliographic coverage. In the bibliography of foreign countries this pattern is a common, although not a universal, one. In using such bibliographies it is well to approach with caution the works of amateur bibliographers. It is important, also, to be aware of the limitations of the general trade bibliography and of the classes of publications, for example, theses and small pamphlets, which it is prone to overlook.

CELLARIUS (Franz). Geographische Unterricht über den Weltthiel von Europa; nebst einem Anhange von ... Amerika. *Eichstadt.* 1787. 8vo. 11656

CELLEM (R.) Visit of His Royal Highness the Prince of Wales to the British North American Provinces and United States in the Year 1860. Compiled from the Public Journals by Robert Cellem. *Toronto.* 1861. 8vo, pp. 438. 11657

CELLIEZ (*Mlle* Adelaide de). Christophe Colomb, suivi d'une nouvelle américaine. *Paris: Gaume frères.* 1840. 2 vols., 8vo. + Nouvelle édition. *Tournai: Casterman.* 1851. 12mo.

CELLIEZ. Christoph Columbus, oder die Entdeckung von Amerika. Nach dem Französischem der Celliez von Joseph Borscht. *Regensburg: Manz.* 1858. 8vo, pp. 348. Engraving. (Bibl. f. die reifere christl. Jugend, xxi. Bd.) 11659

CELLIEZ. Histoire du Paraguay: Par Mlle Celliez. *Paris: Gaume frères.* 1841. 2 vols., 18mo, 12½ sheets. 11660

The Censor. Numb. 1. Saturday, November 23, 1771. [*Boston:*] *E. Russell.* Folio, pp. 4. Continued weekly. BA.

Census. Return of the whole number of Persons within the several Districts of the United States, according to "An Act providing for the Enumeration of the Inhabitants of the United States," passed March 1, one thousand seven hundred and ninty one. *Philadelphia: Printed by Childs and Swaine.* M.DCC.XCI. 8vo, pp. 56. + *London: R. Phillips.* 1793. 8vo, pp. 56. + *Washington.* 1802. 8vo. 11662

Each copy of the Philadelphia edition is signed with the autograph of Thomas Jefferson, at that time Secretary of State. I have not seen the title of the second return. The third is described in the Catalogue of the Library of Congress, thus:

Census of the United States. [Third.] 1810. [*Washington.* 1812?] Oblong folio, 90 l. + *Washington.* [1802?] 8vo.

There is also, "Tabular Statements of the several branches of American Manufactures, exhibiting them by States, Territories and Districts, so far as they are returned in the Reports of the Marshalls, and of the Secretaries of the Territories and their respective Assistants, in the Autumn of the Year 1810, together with similar Returns of Doubtful Goods, Productions of the Soil, and Agricultural Stock, as far as they have been received. *Philadelphia.* 1813." 4to, pp. 50.

Census for 1820, being the Fourth Census. ... *Washington: Printed by Gales and Seaton.* 1821. Folio. 11664

A synopsis of these was printed, *Boston.* 1821. 8vo, pp. 20.

FIGURE 14. SABIN'S DICTIONARY OF BOOKS RELATING TO AMERICA

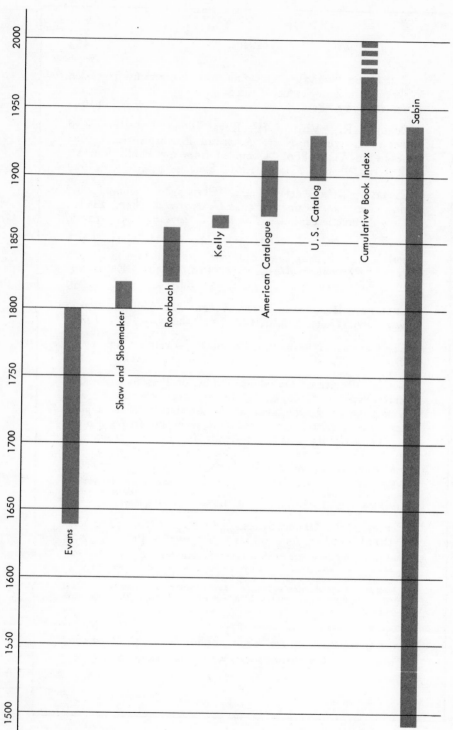

FIGURE 15. CHRONOLOGY OF AMERICAN RETROSPECTIVE BIBLIOGRAPHY

SUGGESTIONS FOR FURTHER INVESTIGATION

I. Outline the retrospective national bibliography of a country which interests you, using as an example the chart in Figure 15.

II. Identify one or more of the following and assess its usefulness to you:
   A. A catalog of the unpublished records of United States government agencies.
   B. Bibliographies of early books published in the individual states of the United States.
   C. A catalog of early books printed in Great Britain.

References for the preceding problems

Collison, Robert L., *Bibliographies: Subject and National.* 2d ed. New York: Hafner Publishing Co., Inc., 1962.

Maclès, Louise-Noëlle, *Les Sources du Travail Bibliographique.* Genève: E. Droz; Lille: Giard, 1950–58. 4 vols.

Pinto, Olga, *Le Bibliografie Nazionali.* 2d ed. Firenze: Olschki, 1951.

Winchell, Constance M., *Guide to Reference Books.* 8th ed. Chicago: American Library Association, 1967; *First Supplement, 1965–1966.* Chicago: American Library Association, 1968.

IV

THE BIBLIOGRAPHY
OF GOVERNMENT PUBLICATIONS

> *. . . the inner workings of the viscera of govern-*
> *ment, which the documents reveal.*
>
> *—John H. Powell*[1]

Because they are not published through ordinary channels, certain classes
of publications tend to escape from the bibliographic net. One of the most
significant of these classes, both in size and in the importance of its content, is that of government publications. Simply defined, a government
publication is any item published at government expense. All levels of
government, from local to national as well as intergovernmental bodies, are
customarily included within this definition. Government publications are
sometimes referred to as public documents, or simply as documents.

Government publications range from the popularly written leaflet to
the highly technical report of research. As the government's involvement in
the lives of its citizens increases, so does the range of its publications. Certainly it would be difficult to find a subject which has not been touched upon
by some form of government publication. Many of these are remarkably
similar to the usual trade publications. Characteristically, however, they
take the form of laws and regulations, decisions, legislative journals, directories, administrative reports, or statistical compilations. No government
could long survive without such records of its work. For the citizen, they
are reliable and relatively unbiased sources of information. For the scholar,
they are primary sources of information. Yet they will not usually be found

---

[1]*Books of a New Nation* (Philadelphia: University of Pennsylvania Press, 1957),
p. 19.

listed in trade bibliographies, nor are they often reviewed in magazines or newspapers. Very few libraries record in their catalogs all the government publications which are in their collections.

Thus, although their importance is unquestioned, government publications tend to form a bibliographic class by themselves. Whatever guides to these publications exist are usually the work of the government concerned. The scholar who seeks a record of the publications of a particular government, therefore, will ordinarily turn to lists issued by that government rather than to a national or trade bibliography. Such government lists may vary as widely as the size, structure, and history of the governments which produce them. The attempt of one government to solve the problem of the orderly presentation of its own records may be seen by the following survey of the bibliography of United States government publications.

CURRENT LISTS: THE UNITED STATES

The chart in Figure 16 shows the traditional division of the government into the legislative, judicial, and executive branches. In the legislative branch, rather surprisingly, is located the Government Printing Office, whose function is the printing, distribution, and sale of government publications. It has been described as the largest job printing shop in the world, and it seems likely that its output exceeds that of any commercial publisher. It has a stock of some 25,000 titles, ranging from inexpensive leaflets to sets of many volumes.

A General List

A list of new titles is issued each month: the *Monthly Catalog of United States Government Publications.*[2] In Figure 17 a page from the issue for January 1968 shows publications which were issued during that month by five government agencies. Each entry is numbered consecutively in the left-hand margin. These publications represent a fair cross section of the forms which government publications may take: reports (654,660), regulations (658), directories (655, 656, 657), a manual (652), and a glossary (659). The bibliographic information for each entry includes the author (the government agency is regarded as the author), title, date, number of pages, and size. The edition, if any, is shown (655). The method to be followed in ordering each publication is indicated by a symbol at the foot of the

---

[2]U.S. Superintendent of Documents, *Monthly Catalog of United States Government Publications* (Washington: Government Printing Office, 1895–date).

THE GOVERNMENT OF THE UNITED STATES

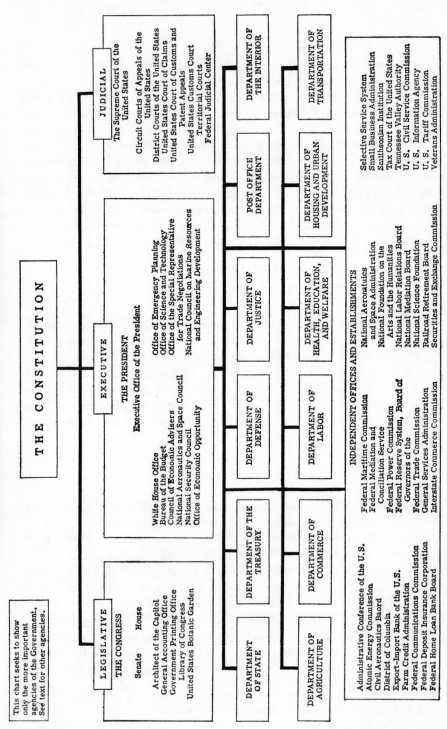

THE CONSTITUTION

This chart seeks to show only the more important agencies of the Government. See text for other agencies.

LEGISLATIVE

THE CONGRESS

Senate   House

Architect of the Capitol
General Accounting Office
Government Printing Office
Library of Congress
United States Botanic Garden

EXECUTIVE

THE PRESIDENT

Executive Office of the President

White House Office
Bureau of the Budget
Council of Economic Advisers
National Aeronautics and Space Council
National Security Council
Office of Economic Opportunity

Office of Emergency Planning
Office of Science and Technology
Office of the Special Representative for Trade Negotiations
National Council on Marine Resources and Engineering Development

JUDICIAL

The Supreme Court of the United States

Circuit Courts of Appeals of the United States
District Courts of the United States
United States Court of Claims
United States Court of Customs and Patent Appeals
United States Customs Court
Territorial Courts
Federal Judicial Center

DEPARTMENT OF STATE
DEPARTMENT OF THE TREASURY
DEPARTMENT OF DEFENSE
DEPARTMENT OF JUSTICE
POST OFFICE DEPARTMENT
DEPARTMENT OF THE INTERIOR
DEPARTMENT OF AGRICULTURE
DEPARTMENT OF COMMERCE
DEPARTMENT OF LABOR
DEPARTMENT OF HEALTH, EDUCATION, AND WELFARE
DEPARTMENT OF HOUSING AND URBAN DEVELOPMENT
DEPARTMENT OF TRANSPORTATION

INDEPENDENT OFFICES AND ESTABLISHMENTS

Administrative Conference of the U.S.
Atomic Energy Commission
Civil Aeronautics Board
District of Columbia
Export-Import Bank of the U.S.
Farm Credit Administration
Federal Communications Commission
Federal Deposit Insurance Corporation
Federal Home Loan Bank Board

Federal Maritime Commission
Federal Mediation and Conciliation Service
Federal Power Commission
Federal Reserve System, Board of Governors of the
Federal Trade Commission
General Services Administration
Interstate Commerce Commission

National Aeronautics and Space Administration
National Foundation on the Arts and the Humanities
National Labor Relations Board
National Mediation Board
National Science Foundation
Railroad Retirement Board
Securities and Exchange Commission

Selective Service System
Small Business Administration
Smithsonian Institution
Tax Court of the United States
Tennessee Valley Authority
U. S. Civil Service Commission
U. S. Information Agency
U. S. Tariff Commission
Veterans Administration

FIGURE 16.   SIMPLIFIED ORGANIZATION CHART OF THE GOVERNMENT OF THE UNITED STATES

FLIGHT STANDARDS SERVICE, Transportation Dept.
Washington, DC 20553

652   Flight test guide: Instrument pilot, airplane. Revised Apr. 1967. [1967.]
vi+13 p. narrow 12° (AC 61–17A.) [Supersedes Sept. 1964 edition.]
* Paper, 10c. ● Item 431–F–3   TD 4.408 : In 7/2

FOREIGN AGRICULTURAL SERVICE, Agriculture Dept.
Washington, DC 20250

[Foreign Agricultural Service miscellaneous], FAS M (series).
653   195. International grains arrangement, 1967. Nov. 1967. [4]+46 p. 4° [Errata,
1 p., issued also.] †
L.C. card Agr 68–23   A 67.26 : 195

654   Report of United States Government to Food and Agriculture Organization of United Nations 1964–66, under art. 11 of FAO constitution ; prepared under auspices of U.S. FAO Interagency Committee [by Ralph W.
Phillips and others]. Oct. 1967. viii+142 p. il. [Title on cover is : U.S.
report to FAO 1964–66.] † ● Item 76–H
L.C. card 55–61390   A 67.35 : 964–66

FOREIGN BROADCAST INFORMATION SERVICE

655   Broadcasting stations of the world [corected to] June 1 ,1967 : pt. 1, Amplitude modulation broadcasting stations, according to country and city.
[21st edition.] cover title, [1]+iii+425+viii p. 4° [Includes world
time chart.] * Paper, $2.25. ● Item 856–B
L.C. card 47–32798   PrEx 7.9 : 967/pt.1

656   ——— pt. 2, Amplitude modulation broadcasting stations according to frequency. [21st edition.] [1967.] cover title, [1]+iii+424+viii p. 4° [In-
cludes world time chart.] * Paper, $2.25. ● Item 856–B
L.C. card 47–32798   PrEx 7.9 : 967/pt.2

657   ——— pt. 3, Frequency modulation broadcasting stations. [21st edition.]
[1967.] cover title, [1]+iii+155+156 p. 4° * Paper, $1.50. ● Item
856–B
L.C. card 47–32798   PrEx 7.9 : 967/pt.3

FOREIGN-TRADE ZONES BOARD
Washington, DC 20230

658   Supplement to June 1966 edition of Laws, regulations, and other information relating to foreign-trade zones in United States. Oct. 1967.
8 p. † ● Item 542
L.C. card 66–62391   FTZ 1.5 : F 76/966/supp.

FOREST SERVICE, Agriculture Dept.
Washington, DC 20250

659   Abridged glossary of terms used in invertebrate pathology ; [by] Edward A.
Steinhaus and Mauro E. Martignoni. 1967. [1]+22 p. 4° (Pacific
Northwest Forest and Experiment Station.) [Includes list of refer-
ences and sourcebooks.] †   A 13.66/2 : P 27

660   Annual fire report for national forests, calendar year 1966. [1967.] [24]
p. il. 4° † (Limited distribution).
L.C. card 68–60203   A 13.32/3 : 966

661   Hydrologic and related characteristics of 3 small watersheds in Oregon
Cascades [with list of literature cited] ; by Jack Rothacher, C. T. Dyr-
ness, Richard L. Fredriksen. 1967. cover title, i+54 p. il. 4° (Pacific
Northwest Forest and Range Experiment Station.) †
L.C. card Agr 68–18   A 13.66/2 : W 29/2

FIGURE 17.   MONTHLY CATALOG OF U.S. GOVERNMENT PUBLICATIONS

page, and the price, if any, is specified. The large black dot followed by the word *Item* and a number indicates that this publication is available to libraries which are depositories for United States government publications. The notation "L.C. card" is followed by the number to be used in ordering Library of Congress catalog cards. The alphanumeric symbol near the right-hand margin of the page is assigned by the Superintendent of Documents and is used in ordering publications from this office. In some libraries these numbers are used as call numbers for the publications. Each issue of the *Monthly Catalog* has an index of titles and subjects. At the end of each year the monthly indexes are cumulated to form an annual index.

A List of the Publications of an Agency

Although it lists some 18,000 publications each year, the *Monthly Catalog* cannot be said to include all United States government publications. It does not index the many bills introduced into each session of Congress, for example, or the multitude of decisions rendered by the federal courts.[3] It is sometimes supplemented by lists issued by individual government agencies for their own publications.[4] Although these lists may in part duplicate the information available in the *Monthly Catalog*, they also offer advantages in convenience of arrangement, depth of indexing, and precise bibliographic description. The *Bureau of the Census Catalog*, a page from which is reproduced in Figure 18, is an example.[5] The notes accompanying each item indicate in detail the contents of the publication, in one entry listing a supplement which is of special interest. (See note under C20, Housing Starts.) A special feature of the *Bureau of the Census Catalog* is a section listing unpublished census information which is available on tape, microfilm, and cards.

---

[3]The Legislative Reference Service of the Library of Congress issues the *Digest of Public General Bills and Selected Resolutions* (Washington: Government Printing Office, 1936–date). *CQ Weekly Report* (Washington: Congressional Quarterly News Features, 1946–date, a non-governmental publication, is helpful in identifying bills, hearings, reports, and other Congressional publications.

The decisions of all but a few courts are issued by commercial publishers rather than by the government. The same is true of the digests, citators, and other aids in tracing court decisions. For a guide to the literature of the law see Miles O. Price and Harry Bitner, *Effective Legal Research* (New York: Prentice-Hall, Inc., 1953).

[4]For a partial list of these see Laurence F. Schmeckebier and Roy B. Eastin, *Government Publications and Their Use*, rev. ed. (Washington: Brookings Institution, 1961), pp. 40–58.

[5]U.S. Bureau of the Census, *Bureau of the Census Catalog* (Washington: Government Printing Office, 1947–date), quarterly, with monthly supplements and annual cumulations.

1960 CENSUS OF HOUSING

†U.S. Census of Housing: 1960—Availability of Published and Unpublished Data

13 pp. Revised February 1966. 25¢.

Describes in outline form the various 1960 housing data that are available in one or more of three forms: (1) printed formal publications; (2) copies of unpublished listings or reproduced statistical tables, almost all of which are also available in the form of microfilm reels; and (3) magnetic computer tape suitable for further summarization and processing on computers compatible with the electronic computers of the Bureau of the Census. Original edition published July 1962.

1960 CENSUSES OF POPULATION AND HOUSING

*1960 Censuses of Population and Housing: Procedural History

393 pp. (June) 1966. $350 (buckram). L.C. Card. No. A65–7414.

See entry under *Population—Publications.*

CURRENT REPORTS

C20 Housing Starts

*Housing Starts in *(month)*

14–20 pp. Monthly. 15¢ per issue; yearly subscription, $1.75 (50¢ additional for foreign mailing). Monthly: November, December 1965; January–October 1966.

Series provides estimates of housing starts, nonfarm and total, including figures for the following: New housing units started, by private and public ownership, with seasonally adjusted annual rate of private starts; by number of housing units in the structure; by metropolitan-nonmetropolitan location; and by Census geographic regions. Periods shown are calendar years beginning 1959 and each month for the last 13–18 months. Cumulative totals to date are also shown for current and preceding year.

The report also includes statistics on new private housing units started (including farm), seasonally adjusted annual rates, by regions, and the number of new private housing units authorized by local building permits in 10,000 and 12,000 permit-issuing places unadjusted and seasonally adjusted annual rate, annually 1959–1963 and for each of the last 12 or more months; seasonal indexes used to adjust private housing starts including farm, and housing units authorized by building permits, by type of structure, for specified months; and average percentage changes and related measures for monthly housing starts and building permit authorizations.

NOTE.—The November 1965 issue includes a special supplement on starts of apartment buildings with 5 or more housing units, second quarter 1964–second quarter 1965.

C25 (Census-HHFA) Housing Sales

†Sales of New One-Family Homes

Monthly, with quarterly supplements and a detailed annual summary. Monthly, 7–8 pp., 10¢ per issue; quarterly, 20–24 pp., 25¢ per issue; annual, price varies. Subscription price including monthly, quarterly, and annual reports, $2.50 per year. Monthly: November, December 1965; January–October 1966. Quarterly (each one report): Third quarter 1964–third quarter 1965; fourth quarter 1964–fourth quarter 1965; first quarter 1965–first quarter 1966; second quarter 1965–second quarter 1966. Annual summary 1965, 88 pp., $1.

Monthly reports provide estimates of sales of new private, nonfarm, one-family homes, current month with revised figures for specified prior months. Statistics are shown on numbers of new homes sold each month and for sale at end of each month, by stage of construction; median number of months from start to sale and from completion to sale, by month of sale; and median number of months since start and since completion of

†Available from Bureau of Census. *Available from GPO. (See p. 2.)

FIGURE 18. BUREAU OF THE CENSUS CATALOG, 1966

A Specialized Index

A publication which supplements the *Monthly Catalog* in a very specialized area is the *U.S. Government Research and Development Reports Index,*[6] a general index to reports of government sponsored research. It indexes reports which appear in *Nuclear Science Abstracts,*[7] *Scientific and Technical Aerospace Reports,*[8] and *U.S. Government Research and Development Reports.*[9] These reports are indexed in five different ways: by subjects, by personal authors, by corporate authors, by contract numbers, and by accession or report numbers. Figure 19 shows a page from the subject index. Each entry here contains the title of the report, the accession or report number, and a reference to the journal in which the item is abstracted. (The letter *N* in the reference indicates *Nuclear Science* Abstracts; *S, Scientific and Technical Aerospace Reports*; and *U, U.S. Government Research and Development Reports.* The numbers following these letters indicate the volume and number of the journal in which the abstract appears.) The price of the report in paper (HC) or microfiche[10] (MF) completes the entry.

RETROSPECTIVE LISTS: THE UNITED STATES

United States government publications have not always received the careful bibliographic treatment that they do today. In the early days of the Republic little thought was given to such matters, and it was not until the burning of the capital in 1814 and the resulting loss of official records that the need for bibliography of government publications began to be felt.[11] Finally, in 1885, a list was assembled, under the supervision of Benjamin Perley Poore, which attempted to bring together the scattered records of the na-

---

[6]U.S. Clearinghouse for Federal Scientific and Technical Information, *U.S. Government Research and Development Reports Index* (Washington: Clearinghouse, 1968–date), semimonthly.

[7]U.S. Atomic Energy Commission, *Nuclear Science Abstracts* (Washington: Government Printing Office, 1948–date), semimonthly.

[8]U.S. National Aeronautics and Space Administration, *Scientific and Technical Aerospace Reports* (Washington: National Aeronautics and Space Administration, 1963–date), semimonthly.

[9]U.S. Clearinghouse for Federal Scientific and Technical Information, *U.S. Government Research and Development Reports* (Washington: Clearinghouse, 1946–date), semimonthly.

[10]A microfiche is a sheet of microfilm.

[11]A very readable account of early United States government publications will be found in *Books of a New Nation,* by J. H. Powell (Philadelphia: University of Pennsylvania Press, 1957).

SUBJECT INDEX

FIGURE 19. U.S. GOVERNMENT RESEARCH AND DEVELOPMENT REPORTS INDEX

tion's early years.[12] If the catalog that Poore and his untrained assistants produced is neither so accurate nor so complete as it might be, it must be remembered that they faced a formidable task in locating and identifying the records of over 100 years. Poore arranged his catalog chronologically, with an index at the end of the volume. Figure 20 shows part of a page for the year 1813 when the war with the British was being fought, not without dissent (see entry for June 29). President James Madison, in his message of May 25, announced that Russia had offered to mediate between the United States and Great Britain. These two publications, like others on this page, were issued as executive documents of the Congress. A good deal of practice and patience is needed to decipher Poore's citations and to trace the publications to which they refer.[13]

Poore's list ended with 1881. It was continued by the *Comprehensive Index* of John G. Ames, which covers the years 1881 through 1893.[14] During these years of growth and expansion, the nation watched with interest the attempts to construct a canal through the Isthmus of Panama. Ames' *Index* shows (Figure 21) some of the reports on this subject issued by the Department of State and the Department of the Navy. In the center column of the page are the titles of the reports, arranged by their key words. (Volume 2 contains an index of personal names.) In the left-hand column are the names of the authors, including government agencies as well as persons. In the column on the right those items which were issued as Congressional publications are identified as either reports, executive documents, or miscellaneous documents of the House or Senate for a particular Congress and session. For example, the report on the Panama Canal by Kimball and Capps was issued as House Miscellaneous Document number 395 of the Forty-ninth Congress, First session. It appears in volume seventeen of these documents and consists of thirty-eight pages. To find this document it is necessary to locate it in the so-called serial set,[15] a collection of Congressional documents each volume of which is identified by a serial number. The table reproduced in Figure 22[16] shows that the report by Kimball and Capps is located in volume 2422.

Ames' index in turn is followed by a publication commonly known as

---

[12]Benjamin Perley Poore, *A Descriptive Catalogue of the Government Publications of the United States, Sept. 5, 1774 to March 4, 1881* (Washington: Government Printing Office, 1885).

[13]An explanation of Poore's citations is given in Schmeckebier and Eastin, *op. cit.*, pp. 9–10.

[14]John Griffith Ames, *Comprehensive Index to the Publications of the United States Government, 1881–1893* (Washington: Government Printing Office, 1905), 2 vols.

[15]Also called the Congressional set, and sometimes known as the sheep set, from the fact that early volumes were bound in sheepskin.

[16]U.S. Superintendent of Documents, *Checklist of United States Public Documents, 1789–1909*, 3d ed. (Washington: Government Printing Office, 1911), p. 77.

Senate Journal, Thirteenth Congress, First Session. May 24, 1813
Printed by R. C. Weightman, Washington. 400 pp.
From May 24, 1813, to August 2, 1813. Vice-President, Elbridge Gerry,* of Massachusetts; Presidents of the Senate pro tempore, Joseph B. Varnum, * of South Carolina, elected December 6, 1813, Joseph Gaillard, of South Carolina, and again elected November 25, 1814; Secretaries of the Senate, Samuel Allyne Otis, of Massachusetts, Charles Cutts, of New Hampshire, elected October 11, 1814.

House Journal, Thirteenth Congress, First Session. May 24, 1813
Printed by A. & G. Way, Washington. 320 pp.
From May 24, 1813, to August 2, 1813. Speakers of the House, Henry Clay, of Kentucky, Langdon Cheves, of South Carolina, elected January 19, 1814; Clerks of the House, Patrick Magruder, of Maryland, Thomas Dougherty, of Kentucky, elected January 30, 1815.

Report of Debates, Thirteenth Congress, First Session. May 24, 1813
Annals of Congress, by Gales & Seaton.
Vol. XXVI, Proceedings, pp. 9-536.

Address to of Senate. Vice-President E. Gerry. 13th Cong., 1st sess., pp. 6-12.
Journal of Senate:
Issues of the present conflict with Great Britain; Efforts of the enemy to disintegrate the Union; Success assured to the American cause if a united and vigorous prosecution of the war is continued; The country in a better condition to cope with the enemy than in the Revolutionary War.

Message from the President of the United States. James Madison. May 25, 1813
Ex. Docs.: 13th Cong. 1st sess. 8 pp.
Russia offers mediation between the United States and Great Britain; Appointment of commissioners to negotiate in accordance with Russia's proposal; Treaty of commerce with Russia; Speculations upon result of friendly interposition by Russia; Untenability of position of British Government in regard to "question of impressment, on which the war so essentially turns;" Search of neutral vessels not sanctioned by law of nations; The methods of warfare adopted by Great Britain criticised; Success of the national forces on land and water; Destruction of a British ship by he Hornet, under Captain Lawrence; Capture of York; Siege of Fort Meigs; Provisions for improving military establishment; Progress of negotiations with France; Death of Minister to France retards arrangements; Finances; Limited revenue; Necessity of a system of internal revenue; Imposition of additional taxes; Patriotic support of Government by the people; Principles of the war.

Executive Reports, Thirteenth Congress, First Session. From May 25, 1813
266 pp.

Washington: A. & G. Way, printers; R. C. Weightman. From May 25, 1813
Executive Documents, Thirteenth Congress, First Session. 20 documents, 394 pp.

Washington: A. & G. Way, printers; Roger C. Weightman, 1813. May 31, 1813
Report on Kaskaskia Land Claims. Commissioner Edward Tiffin.
State Papers: Public Lands, Vol. II, pp. 740,741, 13th Cong.; 1st sess.
Report of the commissioners for the revision of land claims.

Report on Military Pensions. Secretary John Armstrong. June 1, 1813
13th Cong., 1st sess. 47 pp.
Ex. Reports: ... the pension-list ... number of ... in the several

Report on Louisiana Land Claims. Commissioner Edward Tiffin. June 22, 1813
State Papers: Public Lands, Vol. II, pp. 744-871, 13th Cong., 1st sess.
Report of the Commissioners giving the result of their examination of claims in Louisiana.

Further Report on Election of J. P. Hungerford. Rep. James Fisk. June 28, 1813
13th Cong., 1st sess. 2 pp.
Ex. Docs.:
On the petition of John Taliaferro, contesting election of John P. Hungerford. Returns give the sitting member a majority; The contestant claims majority of legal votes on ground that a large number of illegal votes were cast; Examination of qualifications of voters; The spirit and intention of law of Virginia complied with by parties challenged; Committee report that petitioner has not supported his petition.

Remonstrance of the Legislature of Massachusetts against the War. June 29, 1813
Ex. Docs.: 13th Cong., 1st sess. 20 pp.
Massachusetts is opposed to the war with Great Britain; Right and duty of the State to inquire into the grounds and origin of the war, and to promote as far as possible by constitutional means an honorable reconciliation; Powers and duties of the States as parties to the national compact; The alleged causes of war criticised; Their inadequacy asserted; Importance of commerce of the Eastern States; Hostile spirit of non-commercial States to the commerce of the Eastern section; Protection demanded of Congress of commercial interests of the latter; The secrecy of acts of the Administration in relation to foreign affairs deprecated; Protest of a minority of the Legislature to the above remonstrance. Washington: A. & G. Way, printers.

Message on Relations with Sweden. President James Madison. July 6, 1813
State Papers: Foreign Relations, Vol. III, pp. 618-620, 13th Cong., 1st sess.
Appointment by Sweden of a Minister Plenipotentiary to the United States, and nomination of Jonathan Russell to represent the United States in Sweden.

Report on the Militia. Representative George M. Troup. July 8, 1813
Ex. Docs.: 13th Cong., 1st sess. 8 pp.
Inquiry as to alterations necessary in act making provision for arming and equipping the militia; Disposition of the arms purchased for the militia; Amount allotted each State; Provisions of act in regard to their distribution; Principle of distribution; Local necessities regarded; Committee report that present act is ample for ensuring equitable allotment of arms.

Report on Necessary Legislation. Rep. Benson, from joint committee. July 10, 1813
Ex. Docs.: 13th Cong., 1st sess. 2 pp.
List of bills demanding action at present session; Bills relative to the revenue; Bills before the Senate; Bills before the House.

Message on Foreign Relations. President James Madison. July 12, 1813
Ex. Docs.: 13th Cong., 1st sess. 44 pp.
Transmitting information touching the French decree purporting to be a repeal of Berlin and Milan decrees; Report of James Monroe, Secretary of State; Manner in which the first intelligence of the decree of France of April 28, 1811, was received; The information transmitted by Mr. Barlow; No official communication received from France; Cause of failure of France to notify the State Department unexplained; The United States Minister to France is to demand redress of France for every injury ... ask explanation ... holding a ...

FIGURE 20. POORE'S A DESCRIPTIVE CATALOGUE 1774–1881

PALOUSE AND SPOKANE R. R.—PANSEY.

Dubois, F. T., Indian Affairs.	Palouse and Spokane R. R., right of way to, through Nez Perces Reservation, recommended. Mar. 5, 90. H. B. 7509. 26 S. L., 104.	H. R. 51–1, v. 2. No. 645, 1 p.
Court of Claims	Palouse River, memorial of legislature of Washington, praying appropriation for clearing.	S. M. 51–1, v. 2. No. 68, 2 p.
War Department	Pamios, Pierre, admr., findings of court in case of .... Mar. 1, 90. 26 S. L., 1453.	H. M. 51–1, v. 9. No. 127, 2 p.
	Pamlico and Tar rivers, N. C., examination, survey, or improvement of, reports on.— In annual reports of Chief of Engineers, U. S. Army, 1881, p. 1001; 1882, p. 1083; 1883, p. 848; 1884, p. 1036; 1885, p. 1041; 1886, p. 967; 1887, p. 1010; 1888, p. 854; 1889, p. 1044, 1130; 1890, p. 1112; 1891, p. 1347; 1892, p. 1118.	
Davis, R. T., Commerce	Pamlico Point, N. C., establishment of light-house off, recommended .... Mar. 21, 88. H. B. 7421. 25 S. L., 614.	H. R. 50–1, v. 4. No. 1309, 2 p.
Palmer, T. W., Commerce	—— Same .... July 27, 88. H. B. 7421r. 25 S. L., 614.	S. R. 50–1, v. 8. No. 1937, 2 p.
War Department	Pamlico River and Bay River, N. C., waterway between, preliminary examination of, report on. In Annual Rept. of Chief of Engineers, U. S. A., 1891, p. 1421.	
Baker, E. L., consul	Pampas grasses of Argentine Republic, notes on Consular Reports, No. 79, v. 22, p. 505–513, 1 pl. Mar. 26, 87.	H. M. 50–1, v. 21. No. 604.
War Department	Pamunkey River, Va., examination, survey, or improvement of, reports on.— In annual reports of Chief of Engineers, U. S. Army, 1883, p. 819; 1884, p. 992; 1885, p. 982; 1886, p. 917; 1887, p. 942; 1888, p. 828; 1889, p. 1013; 1890, p. 1074; 1891, p. 1275; 1892, p. 1062.	
State Department	Panama Canal, diplomatic correspondence of Geo. Maney, U. S. minister at Bogota, relative to. Mar. 29, 84.	S. M. 48–2, v. 1. No. 12, 8 p.
Rogers, C. C., Navy Department.	—— intelligence report on	H. M. 50–1, v. 6. No. 599, 57 p.
Long, J. D., Representative .	—— Same, res. calling for, from Secretary of Navy .... Mar. 20, 87. 2 m., 23 pl.	H. M. 50–1, v. 6. No. 303, 1 p.
Blaine, J. G., Secretary, State Department.	—— neutrality of, letter relative to .... Mar. 5, 88.	S. E. spcl. sess., 1881. No. 5, 4 p.
Lamar, L. Q. C., Senator	—— progress of work on, reports relative to .... Oct. 22, 81.	S. E. 48–1, v. 6. No. 123, 27 p.
Navy Department.	—— reports on, printing of. (See Public documents.) Mar. 10, 84. 8 ch., 33 pl.	
	—— res. calling for information as to action taken to protect U. S. interests in .... Oct. 13, 81. Rec. 12, 522.	S. M. 47–spcl., v. 1. No. 4, 1 p.
Kimball, W. W., and others.	—— special intelligence report on	H. M. 49–1, v. 17.

FIGURE 21. AMES' COMPREHENSIVE INDEX TO THE PUBLICATIONS OF THE UNITED STATES GOVERNMENT, 1881–1893

Serial no.	Vol.	Part	Series	Document no.	Notes
2418	13	....	H. misc. docs..	180–340.......	Except **273**, in serial no. 2419; **302**, in serial no. 2420; **304 and 305**, both in serial no. 2407, and **338**, in serial no. 2421. 237 is European dock-yards.
2419	14	....	....do........	273............	Rebellion records, series 1, v. 16, pt. 1.
2420	15	....	....do........	302, 379, 380....	Eulogies: Reuben Ellwood, Joseph Rankin, Michael Hahn.
2421	16	....	....do........	338............	Rebellion records, series 1, v. 16, pt. 1.
2422	17	....	....do........	341–395.......	Except **354**, in serial no. 2423; **355**, in serial no. 2424; **371**, in serial no. 2425; **379 and 380**, both in serial no. 2420; **392**, in serial no. 2426, and **393**, in serial nos. 2427 and 2428.
2423	18	....	....do........	354............	American ephemeris and nautical almanac, 1889, 1st ed.
2424	19	....	....do........	355............	Pan-Electric Telephone Company, testimony.
2425	20	....	....do........	371............	Rebellion records, series 1, v. 17, pt. 1.
2426	21	....	....do........	392............	Examination of wools and other animal fibers.
2427	22	1	....do........	393 [pt. 1]......	Lady Franklin Bay expedition (Greely), v. 1, narrative.
2428	22	2	....do........	393, pt. 2......	Same, v. 2, scientific. Contains also 49th Cong. 2d sess., H. misc. doc. 157: Schley's Greely relief expedition.
2429	23	....	....do........	396, pts. 1, 3....	[Monetary or] Silver Commission [of U. S.], 1876; International Monetary conference, Paris, 1881.
2430	24	....	....do........	396, pt. 2......	International Monetary Conference, Paris, 1878.
2431	25	....	....do........	15 [pt. 1]......	Smithsonian Institution, 1885, pt. 1.
2432	26	....	....do........	15, pt. 2.......	Same, pt. 2: National Museum.
2433	27	[1]	....do........	397............	Geological Survey monographs, v. 12: Leadville, Colo.
2434	27	2	....do........	[397]..........	Same, v. 12, atlas.
2435	1	....	H. reports.....	1–373..........	Except **41**, not printed.
2436	2	....	....do........	374–708........	
2437	3	....	....do........	709–1029.......	
2438	4	....	....do........	1030–1276......	1076 relates to Indians and Yellowstone National Park.
2439	5	....	....do........	1277–1542......	Except **1316**, not printed.
2440	6	....	....do........	1543–1887......	Except **1632** and **1680**, not printed.
2441	7	....	....do........	1888–2264......	Except **1931, 1982**, and **1999**, not printed.
2442	8	....	....do........	2235–2577......	
2443	9	....	....do........	2578–2855.....	
2444	10	....	....do........	2856–3142......	Except **2902–2907, 2940**, and **2993**, not printed.
2445	11	....	....do........	3143–3474......	Except **3316**, not printed.
2446	12	....	....do........	3475..........	General personal index of journals of 9th–16th Congresses, being record of Members, 1805–21.

49th CONGRESS, 2d SESSION

Dec. 6, 1886—Mar. 3, 1887

Serial no.	Vol.	Part	Series	Document no.	Notes
2447	....	....	S. journal....	....	
2448	1	....	S. ex. docs....	1–110..........	77 is Taunt's Journey on the Congo in 1885.
2449	2	....	....do........	111–125.......	111 is Shawnee Indian lands; 115 is Chippewa Indians; 117 is Capture of Geronimo; 120 is Count Pulaski, papers, 1777–1884; 125 is Alaska expedition, 1885 (Allen).
2450	1	....	S. misc. docs..	1–29..........	11, 2 pts., is Congressional directory, 2 editions; 15 is Irrigation in U. S. (Hinton).
2451	2	....	....do........	{30, pt. 1....... {31–89, 91......	National Academy of Sciences report, 1886. 53 is Veto messages, 1792–Aug. 4, 1886; 91 is Laws on rivers and harbors, 1790–1887.

FIGURE 22. CHECKLIST OF UNITED STATES PUBLIC DOCUMENTS, 1789–1909

the *Document Catalog*, although its official title is somewhat longer.[17] It is a biennial catalog of subjects, authors, and titles of government publications issued from 1893 through 1940. Figure 23 presents a page from the *Document Catalog* for 1933–1934, years in which the government was concerned with solving the problems of unemployment through such measures as the Civilian Conservation Corps. On this page are listed some of the publications regarding this agency. As in previous indexes the author, title, paging, and size are given. In addition the *Document Catalog* notes illustrations and tables. (See entries for Emergency Conservation Work, *1st and 2d Reports of the Director.*) The descriptions are careful and detailed. (See entries for Emergency Conservation Work, *Safety Division Bulletin*, and for Marsh, C.S., *Educational Program of Civilian Conservation Corps.*) Unlike Poore and Ames, the *Document Catalog* indicates the number of the volume of the serial set in which a given publication appears. For example, the *President's Message on Unemployment Relief* is shown as appearing in three different volumes of this set (9751, 9739, and 9738). In 1940 the *Document Catalog* ceased publication, leaving the *Monthly Catalog*, described earlier, as the only general and comprehensive current index. It continues to list new government publications and to provide monthly and annual indexes to them. Figure 24 shows the sequence of bibliographies which cover United States government publications from 1774 to the present.

BIBLIOGRAPHY OF PUBLICATIONS OF OTHER GOVERNMENTS AND OF INTERGOVERNMENTAL BODIES

In the bibliography of United States government publications it is possible to distinguish three major types of lists: the centralized list of current publications of all agencies, represented by the *Monthly Catalog*; the specialized list issued by an individual agency, such as the *Bureau of the Census Catalog*; and the retrospective bibliography, exemplified by Poore's *Descriptive Catalogue*. A similar pattern may sometimes be discovered at the level of state government (Figure 25). Corresponding to the *Monthly Catalog* at this level is *California State Publications*, a quarterly list with annual cumulations. A representative list issued by an individual state agency is that of the California Division of Mines. A catalog of California state publications for the years 1850 to 1894 corresponds, at the state level, to

---

[17]U.S. Superintendent of Documents, *Catalog of the Public Documents of Congress and of All Departments of the Government of the United States for the Period March 4, 1893–December 31, 1940* (Washington: Government Printing Office, 1896–1945), vols. 1–25.

CIVILIAN CONSERVATION CORPS—Continued.
EMERGENCY CONSERVATION WORK—Continued.

—— President Roosevelt's emergency conservation work program. [1933.] 10 p. il. narrow 8°

—— 1st report of director of emergency conservation work, Apr. 5–Sept. 30, 1933. 1934. v + 63 p. il. 1 tab. [A preliminary report covering the period Apr. 5–Sept. 30, 1933, and including a statistical table of Types of job, appeared as a processed press release, dated Dec. 26, 1933.]

—— 2d report of director of emergency conservation work, Apr. 5, 1933–Mar. 31, 1934. 1934. v + 50 p. il. 5 tab.

—— Safety Division bulletin ECW 1–ECW 23. 4°. [Processed. Some of these Safety Division bulletins are issued in loose-leaf form for insertion in binder. They are superseded by Safety Division regulations, which will appear in a later Document catalog. For contents see **Emergency Conservation Work**.]

LABOR DEPARTMENT. Emergency conservation work bulletin **1** and **3, revised editions.**

1. Chance to work in forests, questions and answers for information of men offered opportunity to apply for national emergency conservation work. Apr. 17, 1933, revised Sept. 25, 1933. [1933.] 7 p.
Same. Apr. 17, 1933, revised Mar. 14, 1934. [1934.]
Same. Apr. 17, 1933, revised June 15, 1934. [1934.]

CIVILIAN CONSERVATION CORPS—Continued.
PRESIDENT OF UNITED STATES—Continued.

—— Executive order, allocating funds to meet emergency and necessity for relief in stricken agricultural areas. June 23, 1934. 1 p. 4° (No. 6747.)

—— Executive order, authorizing relief of certain medical and dental officers of Navy from duty with Civilian Conservation Corps. Jan. 23, 1934. 1 p. 4° (No. 6571.)

—— Executive order, withdrawal of public land for conservation camp, California. Oct. 11, 1933. 1 p. 4° (No. 6331.)

—— Executive order, withdrawal of public lands for flood control purposes, Nevada. Dec. 28, 1933, [published] 1934. 1 p. 4° (No. 6541.)

—— Radio address by President Roosevelt [to Civilian Conservation Corps, July 17, 1933]. [1933.] 1 p. narrow f° ([No.] 120.) [Processed]

—— Unemployment relief, message transmitting request for enactment of the 3 following measures: 1, enrollment of workers now by Federal Government for such public employment as can be quickly started and will not interfere with demand for or proper standards of normal employment; 2, for grants to States for relief; 3, to create broad public works labor creating program. Mar. 21, 1933. 2 p. (H. doc. 6, 73d Cong. 1st sess. In v. 3; **9751.**)

—— Same. (In Congressional record. [Permanent edition.] 1933. v. 77, p. 650 and

FIGURE 23. DOCUMENT CATALOG

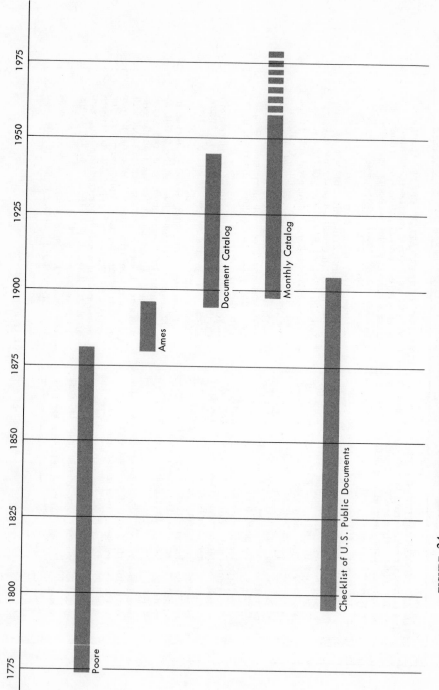

FIGURE 24. CHRONOLOGY OF THE RETROSPECTIVE BIBLIOGRAPHY OF U.S. GOVERNMENT PUBLICATIONS

	NATIONAL	STATE	INTERNATIONAL
Current and Comprehensive	U.S. Superintendent of Documents. *Monthly Catalog of U.S. Government Publications, 1895–date.* Washington: Government Printing Office, 1895–date.	California. State Library. *California State Publications, 1945–date.* Sacramento: State Printer, 1947-date. Monthly with annual cumulations.	United Nations. Dag Hammarskjold Library. Documents Index Unit. *United Nations Documents Index, 1950–date.* New York: United Nations, 1950–date. Monthly, with annual cumulation.
Specialized	U.S. Bureau of the Census. *Bureau of the Census Catalog, 1946–date.* Washington: Government Printing Office, 1947–date.	California. Division of Mines. *Publications of the California Division of Mines to July 1, 1961.* Sacramento: State Printer, 1961.	United Nations. Disarmament Commission. *Index to Documents of the Disarmament Commission . . . 1951–1954.* New York: United Nations, 1953–56. 2 volumes.
Retrospective	Poore, Benjamin Perley. *Descriptive Catalogue of the Government Publications of the United States, Sept. 5, 1774–March 4, 1881.* Washington: Government Printing Office, 1885.	California. Trustees of the State Library. *Catalog of State Publications, 1850–July, 1894.* Sacramento: State Printer, 1895. (In *Report of the Trustees, 1892–94.*)	United Nations. Office of Public Information. *Ten Years of United Nations Publications, 1945–1955.* New York: United Nations, 1955.

FIGURE 25. BIBLIOGRAPHY OF GOVERNMENT PUBLICATIONS: COMMON TYPES WITH EXAMPLES

Poore's retrospective bibliography. At the international level, also, the United Nations follows a similar course, with a current monthly list, the *United Nations Documents Index*; a specialized list of the publications of the United Nations Disarmament Commission; and, as a retrospective bibliography, *Ten Years of United Nations Publications, 1945–1955*.

The wide diversity of the governments of the world is reflected in their publications and in the bibliography which is the orderly presentation of these publications. No one system of government or of bibliography can claim to be truly typical. The preceding survey of the bibliography of United States government publications, therefore, is offered less as a model than as an example of the problems encountered by one government and the solutions which that government has attempted.

SUGGESTIONS FOR FURTHER INVESTIGATION

I. Identify a bibliography of United States government publications other than those described in this chapter. Assess its usefulness to you.

II. Identify a bibliography of government publications for a government other than the United States. You may, if you like, choose the govern- of a city, county, state, or nation. Assess the usefulness of this bibliography to you.

III. Identify a bibliography of the publications of an intergovernmental body. Assess its usefulness to you.

IV. Identify an example of one or more of the following types of aids to the literature of the law. Explain its purpose and use:
A. Legal encyclopedia
B. Annotated code
C. Citator
D. Digest

References for the preceding problems

Boyd, Anne M., *United States Government Publications.* 3d ed., rev. by Rae E. Rips. New York: The H.W. Wilson Co., 1949.

Brimmer, Brenda [and others], *A Guide to the Use of United Nations Documents.* Dobbs Ferry, N.Y.: Oceana Publications, Inc., 1962.

Brown, Everett S., *Manual of Government Publications: United States and Foreign.* New York: Appleton-Century-Crofts, 1950.

Childs, James B., "Bibliographic Control of Federal, State, and Local Documents," *Library Trends*, XV, No. 1 (1966), 13–22.

Etude des Bibliographies Courantes des Publications Officielles Nationales, UNESCO Bibliographical Handbooks, 7, Paris: United Nations Educational, Scientific, and Cultural Organization, 1958.

Price, Miles O. and Harry Bitner, *Effective Legal Research.* New York: Prentice-Hall, Inc., 1953.

Schmeckebier, Laurence F. and Roy B. Eastin, *Government Publications and Their Use,* rev .ed. Washington: The Brookings Institution, 1961.

Yearbook of International Organizations, 1948–date. Brussels: Union of International Associations, 1948–date.

V

LIBRARY CATALOGS:
UNION CATALOGS AND LISTS

Qui scit ubi scientia sit, ille est proximus habenti[1]

In a bibliographic utopia it would be possible to locate quickly and easily a copy of any book in any library in the world. Like the universal register of books, however, the universal library catalog has yet to become a reality. The scholar must still deal with a multiplicity of catalogs, but he need no longer travel to London to consult the catalog of the British Museum or to Paris to scan the treasures of the Bibliothèque Nationale. On the shelves of any large, general research library he will find the published catalogs of many of the world's great libraries. Such catalogs have a value beyond that of making known the contents of particular libraries. Like the national and trade bibliographies described earlier they may serve, when necessary, to describe and identify specific books. On occasion they may also be used as subject indexes to great collections which contain the best of the existing literature in particular subject fields.

PUBLISHED CATALOGS: THE LIBRARY OF CONGRESS

Among the libraries of the United States, the Library of Congress offers the most comprehensive published catalog. The functions of the Library of Congress are broader than its name suggests, for it serves not only the members of Congress but libraries and scholars throughout the nation. Through its Copyright Office it oversees the copyrighting of books, period-

---

[1]Inscribed by Ferdinand Brunetière on his *Manuel de l'Histoire de la Littérature Française.*

icals, music, and films, and it serves as a depository for copyright materials. It maintains a union catalog showing the location of selected books in some 750 North American libraries. It supplies leadership in a huge program to acquire and catalog all scholarly materials published throughout the world. For many years it has printed and sold catalog cards to other libraries. As a further service to scholarship it makes available in book form the catalog of its collection, which in 1969 numbered close to 15,000,000 volumes and pamphlets.

In 1942 the Library of Congress began publication of an author catalog of its collection.[2] A page from this catalog (Figure 26) shows two political pamphlets (see entries for *Frank O. Lowdon, Frank Pierce*), a book in German on soil analysis (Frankau, August), some novels, and a book of poetry (Frankau, Gilbert, *The City of Fear*). In one case both the British and American editions are represented (Frankau, Gilbert, *Christopher Strong*). The entire catalog is reproduced from catalog cards, and each entry carries the bibliographic information normally found on such cards: author, author's dates, title, imprint, number of pages or volumes, size, and notes concerning features such as illustrations or portraits (*Frank O. Lowdon*), or the content or history of the item (*Frank Tousey's Boys Weekly*; Frankau, Gilbert, *The City of Fear*; Frankau, Gilbert, *Gilbert Frankau's Air Ministry, Room 28*). The tracings, by showing what subject entries might be used in a library catalog, give a clue to the subject of the book (see entry for Frankau, August). In general, the bibliographic information given here follows the pattern of that for new books listed in *Publishers' Weekly*.

Included in this catalog are all items cataloged by the Library of Congress: books, periodicals, music, phonorecords, motion pictures, and filmstrips. (Some of these were later listed in separate catalogs.)[3] Also included are certain books held by other government libraries. For example, the book by August Frankau in Figure 26 is located in the U.S. Department of Agriculture Library, as indicated by the note in the lower left-hand corner of the card. Except for anonymous works such as the pamphlets and the

[2]U.S. Library of Congress, *A Catalog of Books Represented by Library of Congress Printed Cards Issued to July 31, 1942* (Ann Arbor, Michigan: J.W. Edwards Publisher, Inc., 1942–46), 147 vols. This was followed by *Supplement: Cards Issued August 1, 1942–December 31, 1947* (Ann Arbor, Michigan: J.W. Edwards Publisher, Inc., 1948), 42 vols., and by *Library of Congress Author Catalog: A Cumulative List of Works Represented by Library of Congress Printed Cards, 1948–52* (Ann Arbor, Michigan: J.W. Edwards Publisher, Inc., 1953), 24 vols. It is continued by the *National Union Catalog*.

[3]U.S. Library of Congress, *Library of Congress Catalog—Music and Phonorecords* (Washington: Library of Congress, 1953–date), semi-annual with cumulations; and U.S. Library of Congress, *Library of Congress Catalog—Motion Pictures and Filmstrips* (Washington: Library of Congress, 1953–date), quarterly with cumulations; also *New Serial Titles*, which will be described later in this chapter.

Frankau, August.

Untersuchungen uber die beziehungen der physikalischen bodeneigenschaften zueinander und zur mechanischen boden-analyse ... Straubing, C. Attenkofer'sche buch- und kunst-druckerei, 1909.

3 p. l., 46 p. 22^{cm}.

Inaug.-diss.–K. Technische hochschule zu Munchen.
Bibliographical foot-notes.

1. Soils–Analysis. [1. Soil–Analysis] 2. [Soil physics]

Agr 15–539

U.S. Dept. of agr. Library	57F85
for Library of Congress	[a41b1]

Frankau, Gilbert, 1884–

Gilbert Frankau's Air Ministry, room 28. New York, E.P. Dutton & co., inc., 1942.

383 p. 20½^{cm}.

"First edition."
"Published in England under the title Winter of dis-content."

1. European war, 1939–   –Fiction.   I. Title: Air ministry, room 28.

41–26740

Library of Congress	PZ3.F85A1
	[20]

Frankau, Gilbert, 1884–

... Christopher Strong, a romance. London, Hutchinson & co., ltd. [1932]

384 p. 19½^{cm}.

I. Title.

32–7915

Library of Congress	PZ3.F85Ch
Copyright A ad int. 16133	[3]

Frankau, Gilbert, 1884–

... Christopher Strong, a romance. New York, E.P. Dutton & co., inc. [^{c}1932]

384 p. 19½^{cm}.

"First edition."

I. Title.

32–20042

Library of Congress	PZ3.F85Ch 2
————Copy 2.	
Copyright A 53559	[5]

Frankau, Gilbert, 1884–

The city of fear, and other poems, by Gilbert Frankau. London, Chatto & Windus, 1918.

5 p. l., 3–48 p. 21^{cm}.

"Includes a reprint of 'The guns ... ' thus forming a complete collection of Gilbert Frankau's war-poetry."–Note.
"Third impression, February, 1918."

1. European war, 1914–   –Poetry.   I. Title.

19–5931

Library of Congress	PR6011.R26C5 1918
	[4]

Frankau, Gilbert, 1884–

Dance, little gentleman! By Gilbert Frankau. London, Hutchinson & co. ltd. [1929]

320 p. 19½^{cm}.

I. Title

29–23894

Library of Congress	PZ3.F85Dan
Copyright A ad int. 13105	[2]

60

Frankau, Gilbert, 1884–

Dance, little gentleman! By Gilbert Frankau. New York and London, Harper & brothers, 1930.

319 [1] p. 20^{cm}.

"First edition."

I. Title

30–2371

Library of Congress	PZ3.F85Dan2
————Copy 2.	
Copyright A 17953	[3]

Frankau, Gilbert, 1884–

The dangerous years; a trilogy, by Gilbert Frankau. London, Hutchinson & co., ltd. [1937]

686 p. 19^{cm}.

CONTENTS.–Pre-war.–Post-war.–Present day.

I. Title.

37–35065

Library of Congress	PZ3.F85Dao
Copyright A ad int. 23138	[5]

Frankau, Gilbert, 1884–

The dangerous years, a trilogy by Gilbert Frankau. New York, E.P. Dutton & co., inc. 1938.

7 p. l., 13–686 p. 20½^{cm}.

"First edition."
CONTENTS.–Pre-war.–Post-war.–Present day.

I. Title.

38–27041

Library of Congress	PZ3.F85Dao2
————Copy 2.	[5]

Frankau, Gilbert, 1884–

... Everywoman. London, Hutchinson & co., ltd. [1933]

ix, 11–448 p. 19½^{cm}.

At head of title: A novel by Gilbert Frankau.

I. Title.

33–23924

Library of Congress	PZ3.F85Ev
Copyright A ad int. 18137	[3]

FIGURE 26. A CATALOG OF BOOKS REPRESENTED BY LIBRARY OF CONGRESS PRINTED CARDS ISSUED TO JULY 31, 1942 [U.S. Library of Congress, *Catalog of Books Represented by Library of Congress Printed Cards Issued to July 31, 1942* (Ann Arbor, Michigan: J. W. Edwards Publisher, Inc., 1942–46), vol. 51, p. 60. Used by permission of the publisher.]

periodical, the entries on this page are arranged by the names of their authors. Those by the same author are arranged under his name by their titles. In 1950 the publication of a current subject catalog was begun.[4] A page from this catalog, reproduced in Figure 27, shows some of the books on narcotics which were cataloged for the library between 1950 and 1954. German, Egyptian, Czech, and French publications are represented, as well as reports of international agencies such as the International Criminal Police Commission and the United Nations. This subject catalog serves not only as an index to the books cataloged by the Library of Congress but also, because of the breadth of this library's collection, as a guide to the existing literature on a wide variety of topics.

PUBLISHED CATALOGS OF OTHER LIBRARIES

Even more useful on occasion than the catalogs of large general libraries like the Library of Congress are those of smaller and more specialized collections, such as the subject catalog of the Peabody Museum of Archaeology and Ethnology.[5] A page from this catalog (Figure 28) shows a part of the collection on Tibet, including not only books but also articles from appropriate journals. New developments in the technology of printing have made possible the reproduction in book form of many such libraries and collections. A list of some of these appears at the end of this chapter.

UNION CATALOGS

Such catalogs represent a large step toward making the contents of the world's libraries widely available. A further step in this direction was the creation of the union catalog, which combined the catalogs of a group of libraries. The idea is not new. Goethe is said to have proposed such a catalog for the libraries of Weimar as early as 1798. Charles Evans, when he included in his *American Bibliography* the names of libraries having copies of the books he listed, was approaching the idea of a union catalog. The Library of Congress catalog, by including titles held by other government libraries, was also tending in this direction. In fact, a union catalog, on cards, has existed for many years within the Library of Congress. It was

---

[4]U.S. Library of Congress, *Library of Congress Catalog—Books: Subjects* (Washington: Library of Congress, 1950–date), quarterly with cumulations.

[5]Harvard University, Peabody Museum of Archaeology and Ethnology, *Library Catalogue* (Boston: G.K. Hall & Co., 1963), 54 vols. (Part 1, *Authors*, Part 2, *Subjects*).

NARCOTICS (Continued)

Carnegie Endowment for International Peace.

Narcotic drug control. Introd. by Herbert L. May. [Anne Winslow, editor] New York [1952] 489-536 p. map. 20 cm. (International conciliation. Nov. 1952, no. 485)
JX1907.A8 no. 485 *614.3 178.8   53–1041
————Copy 3.   HV5801.C35

Heubner, Wolfgang, 1877–

Genuss und Betaubung durch chemische Mittel. Berlin, Akademie Verlag, 1948.
38 p. 21 cm. (Deutsche Akademie der Wissenschaften zu Berlin; Vortrage und Schriftem, Heft 25)
QP456.H48   51–28110

Heubner, Wolfgang, 1877–

Genuss und Betaubung durch chemische Mittel. Wiesbaden, Verlag fur Angewandte Wissenschaften, 1952.
38 p. 21 cm.
QP456.H48 1952   52–33054 †

Indiana. *Dept. of Education.*

A course of study on effects of alcoholic beverages, tobacco, sedatives and narcotics upon the human body. [Indianapolis] B. H. Watt, state superintendent of public instruction, 1948.
iv, 24 p. 23 cm.   Bulletin no. 201)
HV5060.I 55 1948   178.0712772   48–47614*

International Criminal Police Commission.

Memorandum au sujet du trafic illicite des stupefients. 1949/50–
[New York]
v. 28 cm. (Nations Unles. [Document] E/CN.7)
JX1977.A212   *614.3 178.8   53–4026
——— ————2d set.   HV5800.U449

League of Nations. *Advisory Committee on Traffic in Opium and Other Dangerous Drugs.*

Analytical study of annual reports by governments on the traffic in opium and other dangerous drugs for the year 1940. [Geneva, 1945]
40 p. 33 cm. (Series of League of Nations publications. xi. Opium and other dangerous drugs. 1945.xi.2)
JX1975.A25 1945.xi.2   178.8   50–3080
——— ————Copy 2. JX1975.A2 1945.C.117.M.117.xi
——— ————Copy 3. HV5801.L4   1940b

Maurer, David W.

Narcotics and narcotic addiction, by David W. Maurer [and] Victor H. Vogel. Springfield, Ill., Thomas [1954]
xv, 303 p. illus. 24 cm. (American lecture series, publication no. 169. A Monograph in the Bannerstone division of American lectures in public protection)
RC566.M3   *616.86 178.8   53–10953

Oursler, William Charles, 1913–

Narcotics: America's peril, by Will Oursler and Laurence Dwight Smith. [1st ed.] Garden City, N. Y., Doubleday, 1952.
284 p. 22 cm.
HV5825.O8   *364.1 178.8   52–8751 †

Rice, Thurman Brooks, 1888–

Effects of alcoholic drinks, tobacco, sedatives, narcotics, by Thurman B. Rice and Rolla N. Harger. Chicago, Wheeler Pub. Co. [1949]
viii, 312 p. illus. 21 cm.
HV5060.R5   1952   612.01446   50–5090

Rice, Thurman Brooks, 1888–

Effects of alcoholic drinks, tobacco, sedatives, narcotics, by Thurman B. Rice and Rolla N. Harger. Rev. ed. Chicago, Wheeler Pub. Co. [1952]
312 p. illus. 21 cm.
HV5060.R5   1952   612.01446   52–42180 †

Rolin, Jean.

Drogues de police. Paris, Plon [1950]
306 p. 19 cm.   (Presences)
RA1056.R6   340.6   50–30628

Russell, *Sir* **Thomas Wentworth, 1879–**

Egyptian service, 1902-1946. [1st ed.] London, Murray [1949]
ix, 294 p. plates, ports, maps. 23 cm.
HV8269.A2R8   923.542   50–31646

United Nations.

Liste des entreprises autorisees a fabriquer des stupefiants tombant sous le coup de la Convention. Application de l'article 20 de la Convention pour limiter al fabrication et reglementer la distribution des stupefiants, signee le 13 juillet 1931 et amendee par le Protocole du 11 decembre 1946. New York, 1953.
39 p. 28 cm. (Nations Unies. [Document] E/NF.19-53/1)
JX1977.A212 E/NF.1953/1 *614.3 178.8 54–253

[United Nations]

Narcotic durgs; international control of drugs outside the scope of the Convention of July 13, 1931, as amended. Protocol between the United States of America and other Governments dated at Paris November 19, 1948 ... Proclaimed by the President of the United States of America January 10, 1951, entered into force with respect to the United States of America September 11, 1950. [Washington, U. S. Govt. Print. Off., 1952]
48 p. 24 cm. (U. S. Dept of State. Publication 4389. Treaties and other international acts series, 2308)
JX235.9.A32 no. 2308 *614.3 178.8 52–61173

[United Nations]

Protocol bringing under international control drugs outside the scope of the Convention of July 13, 1931, for limiting the manufacture and regulating the distribution of narcotic drugs as amended by the Protocol of 11th December, 1946. Paris, 19th November, 1948. London, H. M. Stationery Off. [1950]
21 p. 25 cm. ([Gt. Brit. Foreign Office. Treaty series, 1950, no. 4)
JX636   1892   1950, no. 4   178.8   50–3532

United Nations.

Protocol on narcotic drugs; protocol amending the agreements, conventions and protocols on narcotic drugs concluded at The Hague on 23 January 1912, at Geneva on 11 February 1925 and 19 February 1925 and 13 July 1931, at Bangkok on 27 November 1931 and at Geneva on 26 June 1936. Protocole sur les stupefiants; protocole amendant les accords, conventions et protocoles sur les stupefiants conclus a La Haye le 23 janvier 1912, a Geneva le 11 fevrier 1925 et le 19 fevrier 1925 et le 13 julliet 1931, a Bangkok le 27 novembre 1931 et a Geneve le 26 juin 1936. Lake Success, 1947.
8 p. 31 cm.
HV5801.U47   178.8   49–885 rev*

United Nations.

Protocolo sobre estupefacientes; protocolo enmendando los acuerdos, convenios y protocolos sobre estupefacientes concertados en La Haya el 23 de enero de 1912, en Ginebra el 11 de febrero de 1924, el 19 de febrero de 1925 y el 13 de julio de 1931, en Bangkok el 27 de noviembre de 1931 y en Ginebra el 26 de junio de 1936. Lake Success, 1937.
5 p. 32 cm.
HV5801.U473   178.8   50-931

United Nations. *Drug Supervisory Body.*

Evaluaciones de las necesidades mundiales de estupefacientes. Ginebra.
v. 32 cm. annual. (Naciones Unidas. [Documento] E/DSB)
JX1977.A213   178.8   51–7049
——— ————2d set.   HV5800.U447

FIGURE 27. LIBRARY OF CONGRESS CATALOG. BOOKS: SUBJECTS [U.S. Library of Congress, *Library of Congress Catalog. Books: Subjects* (Ann Arbor, Michigan J. W. Edwards Publisher, Inc., 1954) vol. 13, p. 349. Used by permission of the publisher.]

L.SOC.48.85.20 vol.15
 	
Tibet.
 	
Bailey, F   M
 	
  The story of Kintup.
 	
  (In The Geographical magazine. London,1943.
v.XV,p.426-431,illus.,port.,map)
	AS. C 548 m
	
	Tibet.
	
	Clark,Leonard
	  The marching wind. New York,Funk and
	Wagnalls Company,1954.
	  xvi,368 p. front.,plates,maps. 23 cm.

L.SOC.48.85.16 vol.63
 	
Tibet.
 	
Bell, (Sir) C.
 	
  A year in Lhasa.
 	
  (In the Geographical journal.London,1924.
v.LXIII, p.89-101, illus.)
	Tibet L.SOC. 48.85.16 vol.53
	
	Coales, O.
	
	  Eastern Tibet.
	
	London, 1919.
	
	  (In the Geographical journal. vol.LIII,
	p.228-253, illus.)

AS. B 541 a
 	
Tibet.
 	
Bishop, Isabella L
 	
  Among the Tibetans...,London,The Religious
tract society,1894. 159 p. front.,illus.
19 cm. (The Leisure hour library. New series)
	MUS.120.31.5.1 vol.37
	Tibet.
	
	Cutting,O Suydam
	
	  In Lhasa, the forbidden. An extraordinary
	trip to a city which few explorers have reached
	where the palace-monastery of the Dalai Lama
	stands supreme.
	
	  (In Natural history. New York,1936. v.XXVII,
	p.102-126,illus.,map,facsims.)

AS. B 644 deE
Tibet.
 	
Bonvalot, Gabriel
 	
  Across Thibet; being a translation of "De
Paris au Tonkin a travers le Tibet inconnu,"
by Gabriel Bonvalot...Translated by C.B.Pitman
...London,Melbourne, etc.,Cassell & company,
limited,1891. 2 v. front., illus.,ports.,fold.
map. 25 cm.
	L.SOC.120.35.4 vol.26
	Tibet.
	
	David-Neel, Alexandra
	
	  Lhasa at last,a revelation of hidden
	mysteries and curious customs at the Tibetan
	capital.
	
	  (In Asia. New York,1926. v.XXVI,p.624-633,
	644-646,illus.)

AS. B 664 i
Tibet.
 	
Boulnois, Helen Mary
 	
  Into little Thibet...London,Simpkin,Marshall,
Hamilton,Kent & Co.,ltd.,1923. 256 p. front.,
plates (part col.),tab.,diagrs. 19 cm.
	L.SOC.120.35.4 vol.26
	Tibet.
	
	David-Neel, Alexandra
	
	  Lost in Tibetan snows...
	
	  (In Asia. New York,1926. V.XXVI,p.428-435,
	452-454,illus.,maps)

FIGURE 28. THE SUBJECT CATALOG OF THE PEABODY MUSEUM OF ARCHAEOLOGY AND ETHNOLOGY [Harvard University, Peabody Museum of Archaeology and Ethnology, Library, *Catalogue* (Boston: G. K. Hall & Co., 1963), *Subjects*, vol. 26, p. 512. Used by permission of the publisher.]

begun in 1901, when the Library of Congress began to distribute depository sets of its printed cards to selected libraries in order to make the record of its holdings widely available. Some of these depository libraries, among them Harvard University Library, the New York Public Library, the Boston Public Library, and the John Crerar Library, reciprocated by sending copies of their own cards to the Library of Congress, where they formed the nucleus of a union catalog. In 1927, under a grant from John D. Rockefeller, this catalog was greatly expanded. In 1956 the current additions to the union catalog were combined with the current author catalog of the Library of Congress and issued as the *National Union Catalog*.[6] This publication, whose function as a current national bibliography was described in Chapter 2, serves also as a union catalog and lists, in addition to books cataloged by the Library of Congress, many rare and unusual items reported by some 750 other North American research libraries. On the page shown in Figure 7, the symbols in the lower left-hand corner of some of the catalog cards indicate the libraries that hold copies of the items listed. (See entries for Brewton, Bricaud, Briceño.)

Thus, from 1956 to the present, the *National Union Catalog* has made accessible the records of books being added to the major North American research libraries. The earlier part of this union catalog is still in card catalog form, with the exception of those titles published between 1952 and 1955 which were reported to the union catalog by the contributing libraries. These have been published in a set of thirty volumes.[7] The entire union catalog, from the beginning to 1956, is being published in a set estimated to run to 600 volumes. Although it is undoubtedly the largest union catalog in the United States, the National Union Catalog is by no means the only one. Libraries of individual cities or regions may maintain combined catalogs. By including small, out-of-the-way libraries or collections, these local catalogs serve as supplements to the *National Union Catalog*.

UNION LISTS

Also supplementing the *National Union Catalog* are various union lists, each confined to special materials such as newspapers, microfilms, serials, theses, or periodicals. The foremost example of a union list in the United States and Canada is the massive *Union List of Serials*, which in five large

---

[6]For a summary of the rather complex history of the *National Union Catalog* see Constance M. Winchell, *Guide to Reference Books*, 8th ed. (Chicago: American Library Association, 1967), pp. 7–8.

[7]*National Union Catalog: 1952–1955 Imprints* (Ann Arbor, Michigan: J.W. Edwards, Publisher, Inc., 1961), 30 vols.

volumes lists and locates over 156,000 serials.[8] A serial is any publication which is issued in successive parts. It is usually meant to be continued indefinitely, in contrast to a work that is meant to be complete in a certain number of volumes. Serials include, then, such important forms as journals, memoirs, proceedings, and annual reports. The page from the *Union List of Serials*, reproduced in Figure 29, lists both a monthly periodical (*Ballet, London*) and a yearbook (*Ballet Annual*). The symbols following each entry indicate the libraries where files of a particular serial are available and the volumes held by each. For example, library AAP (Auburn University) holds volume 11 of the *Ballet Annual*; ArU (University of Arizona) holds volume 13; C and CL (California State Library and Los Angeles Public Library) have complete files beginning with volume 1. Only one library, CtY (Yale), holds *Ballroom and Band*. That this is an incomplete file of volume 1 is indicated by [1].

The *Union List of Serials*, however, does more than locate files of serials. It also shows which serials have ceased publication (indicated in Figure 29 by ‖ following the date, see *Balloon*) and which were still being published (indicated by + following the date, see *Ballroom and Band*). The place of publication and date of the first volume are given, and also the date of the last volume if the serial has ceased publication. Note is made of supplements (*Ballroom and Band*) and changes of title (*Ballou's Monthly Magazine*). If the serial has ever suspended publication, this fact is noted (*Ballet, London; Ballon*). Because of the bibliographic information which it supplies, the *Union List of Serials* is used to describe and identify serials in much the same way that the *National Union Catalog* or the *Cumulative Book Index* is used to describe and identify books. The page shown in Figure 29, for example, might be used to distinguish between two periodicals both of which are called *Ballet* and both of which are published in London, but for which the *Union List of Serials* reveals different dates.

No title on the page shown in Figure 29 begins publication later than 1947. A search through the entire work would reveal none beginning later than 1949. In 1950 the task of describing and locating new serials was taken over by a Library of Congress publication. *New Serial Titles*.[9] The bibliographic information given in this publication (Figure 30) follows the pattern set by the *Union List of Serials*. An additional feature is the classification number at the head of each entry to indicate the subject area of each new serial. Together the *Union List of Serials* and *New Serial Titles* include the holdings of almost 1,000 libraries in the United States and

---

[8]*Union List of Serials in Libraries of the United States and Canada*, 3d ed. (New York: The H.W. Wilson Co., 1965), 5 vols.

[9]*New Serial Titles: A Union List of Serials Commencing Publication After December 31, 1949* (Washington: Library of Congress, 1950–date), monthly with cumulations.

BALLETOMANE. (San Francisco ballet guild) San Francisco. 1,summer 1949+
NN 1+

BALLI kombetar. *See* Flamuri

BALLITORE magazine consisting of original pieces and communications. Dublin. 1820-21‖
1U no1-4,Ap-Jl 1820

BALLON. Bulletin trimestriel de toutes les ascensions. Paris. 1-6,1878-Ja/F/Mr 1883‖?
Suspended My 1879-Mr 1880; My-S 1880. Subtitle varies
CtY [3]   MCM [1-6]
DLC 1-[4-6]

BALLON poste; journal du siège de Paris, publié pour les départements et l'étranger. Paris. no1-22,O 30 1870-Ja 29 1871‖
DLC   NN

BALLOON; or Aërostatic magazine. London. v1 no1-4,Ag-D 1845‖
CSmH v1 no1   MCM
DLC v1 no1-2   MH
MB v1 no1

BALLOON pictorial. N.Y. v1 no1,Jl 1866‖?
DLC no1   MWA no1

BALLOONING and aeronautics. London. no1-6,Ja-Je 1907‖
DLC   MCM
ICJ

BALLOT box. *See* National citizen and ballot box

BALLOU bulletin board. (Ballou family association of America) Waterbury. 1,D 1946+
Ct 1+   MnHi 1+
DLC [1]   NN 1+
MeHi 1+

BALLOU family association of America Proceedings. Providence. 1-4,1908-11‖?
CtY 1   N 1,3-4
DLC 1   WHi 1
MnHi 1,3

See also Ballou bulletin board

BALLOU'S monthly magazine. Boston. 1-77, 1841-93‖?
1841-Ap 1863 as Ballou's dollar monthly magazine; My 1863-Ja 1865 Dollar monthly magazine
CaL [27,30,36]-46   MoS 15,17-18,21,23
Ct [5-7]75-77   N [1]-9,11-15,17-[20]-
CtHW 5-8,12,17-30,   30[51-52]
33-34   NBu [47-49]
CtY [4-68]   NBuG 23-24,35,54-55,
DLC [1-75]   59
IC 69-77   NN 1-[8-38]-77
IChi 8,15-17   NPV [2]3,17-18,21-22,
ICN [2-77]   25-26
ICU 47-50   NR 3-5,23
InI 31-50   NSU 1-2,4-5
InS 23,75-76   NjR [1-67]
KyBB 39   OC 33-35,37-48
LNHT [5-36]   OCl 3,6,11-19,25-32
MB 1-15[21-76]   41-47,61-63
MBAt 8-11   OClWHi [9-33]
MBC 8,12   OO [11-65]
MH [3-40]-54   OT 31-32
MNF [1,3,19]25-50   OU 23-24,27-28
MWA [1-65]   PP [5]-8,25-26
MdBE [5-26]   PU [24]-[26]
MeB [33-49]   RPB [3-77]
MiD-B [8,25]47-48   TxU [1-47]
MiU [2-38]-40,51-54   VU [40]-[53]
MnU [1-44]   VW [32,34-35,37]
MoK 65-68,71-74   WHi [1-47]

CtHW 5-8,12,17-34   N [1]-9,11-[20]-32,
MdBP 5   39-46[51-52]
MoU 25-62   NhD 37-38
        WM 13-15,17-20,25-27

BALLOU'S pictorial drawing-room companion. Boston. 1-17,My 3 1851-D 24 1859‖
1-7,1851-54 as Gleason's pictorial drawing-room companion
C 1,4-9   Ct 1-9
CSd 1-3   CtHW 1-[15]
CSmH 3,6-9   DLC
CU   ICN 1-15,17
CaH [11,13]   ICR 6-7
CaL 4-[6-7]8,10   ICU [4-5,8-9,11,16]
CaT   IEN 3-10
CoD 2-7   IU 1-13

Ia 1-14,16-17   NN 1-16
8-14,16-17   6-7

BALLROOM and band. London. 1, N 1934+
Each issue accompanied by supplement: Rhythm record review
CtY [1]

BALLYHOO. N.Y. v1-16 no1, Ag 1931-F 1939‖?
DLC   NN [1]-[15]
MnU 1-2   VU [1-2, 4]

BALM of Gilead and practical universalist. Concord, N.H. v1-4 no24,Jl 16 1842-Ag 9 1845‖?
CaL 1   MiU-C [4]
ICM 1-[3]   NCaS 1
MB 1[2]   Nh v1 no52
MMeT 1   NhM 1[2-3]
MWA [1-2]-4   N I

BALNEOLOGE; zeitschrift für die gesamte ⊗ physikalische und diätetische therapie. ▲ (Deutsche gesellschaft für bäder- und klimakunde; Deutsche gesellschaft für rheumabekämpfung; Standesverein der reichsdeutschen badeärzte) Berlin. v1-11 no4/6,Ja 1934-Ap/Je 1944‖

Supersedes Zeitschrift für physikalische therapie
CSt-L 1+   IaAS 1+
CtY 1+   MBM 1+
DSG 1-34   MWhB 1+
DWB 5+   MnRM 1+
ICJ [1]   MnU 1+
ICU 1+   NNN 1+

BALNEOLOGIE und balneotherapie. *See* Internationaler aerztlicher fortbildungskursus

BALNEOLOGISCHE beiblätter. See Ärztliche mitteilungen

BALNEOLOGISCHE gesellschaft, Berlin Veröffentlichungen. 1,1879+
1-10,1879-88 as Gesellschaft für heilkunde in Berlin, Balneologische section. Veröffentlichungen; 11-29,1889-1908 Hufelandsche gesellschaft in Berlin. Veröffentlichungen öffentliche versammlungen der Balneologischen gesellschaft
CSt-L 36-39,41-43   MBM 2-35
CaM 16-17,24-28   MH 34
DLC 31-32
DSG 1,4-5,9,11-34   NNN 1-2,10-11,14,
ICJ 15-19,21,26-35   17-19,22-35

BALNEOLOGISCHE zeitung. (Deutsche gesellschaft für hydrologie) Wetzlar. 1-11,Ja 1855-Mr 1862‖
Superseded by Archiv für balneologie
CSt-L 1,3[5]   NBM 2,5-7,
DLC   NNN
DSG   PPC
MBM 1-7[9-11]

BALNEOLOGISCHE zeitung. (Verein der kurorte und mineralquellen-interessenten Deutschlands, Oesterreich-Ungarns und der Schweiz) Berlin. 1-13,1890-1902‖?
DSG 5-13

BALNEOLOGISCHE centralzeitung. (Allgemeiner deutscher bäderverband und Schwarzwaldbadertag) Berlin. 1-8,1900-07‖
Supplement to Medicinische woche
CSt-L [2-7]   NNN 1-7
DSG   PPC 2-7
MBM [1]-8

BALNEOLOGISCHES centralblatt. Leipzig. v1-3 no1,O 1890-O 7 1892‖
DSG   NNN [1-2]3
ICJ   PPC [1-2]3
NNC-M 1-2

BALT-press. Stockholm. Bulletin no1,Ap 5 1946+
DLC 1-17

BALTENLAND berichte. Danzig.
CtY [1938-39]   MH [1938-39]
DLC [1938-39]   WaU [1938-39]
        ICMiLC c 1938-39;

BALTIC and Scandinavian countries. (Baltic institute) Thorn; Leyden; etc.
v1 5   Ap 1939‖

NEW SERIAL TITLES

SUPERSEDES IN PART ACADEMIA REPUBLICII POPULARE ROMINE. SCIENCE DANS LA REPUBLIQUE POPULAIRE ROUMAINE, AND CONTINUES ITS VOLUME NUMBERING. SUPERSEDED IN 1956 BY REVUE DE PHYSIQUE AND REVUE DE MATHEMATIQUES PURES ET APPLIQUEES. TEXT IN FRENCH, GERMAN OR ENGLISH.

```
C U            CA OON
D LC           I U
IN LP          M CM
M H            MD BJ
MI U           MO KL
N N            N NC
N NU           R PB
W U
```

REVUE DE MATHEMATIQUES PURES ET APPLIQUEES. [ACADEMIA REPUBLICII POPULARE ROMINE] BUCHAREST. 1 1956-
SUPERSEDES IN PART REVUE DE MATHEMATIQUES ET DE PHYSIQUE. TEXT IN FRENCH, GERMAN OR ENGLISH.

510
```
C LU [1-5]-    CA QTU 1-
CA OON 1-      D LC [1]-
CT Y 1-        IA AS 1-
IN U 1-        KY CM 1-
K U 1-         M CM [1]
L U 1-         MD BJ 1-
M H 1-         MN U 1-
MI U [1]       N IC 1-
MO KL 1-       N N 1-
N NBELL 1-     N NU 1-
N NC 1-        O U 1-
N JP [4]-      R PB 1-
TX HR 1-       WA U 1-
W U 1-
```

REVUE DE MECANIQUE APPLIQUEE. [ACADEMIA REPUBLICII POPULARE ROMINE. INSTITUTUL DE MECANICA APLICATA] BUCHAREST. 1, 1956-
SUPERSEDES IN PART REVUE DES SCIENCES TECHNIQUES.

620.1   621
```
A AP 1-        C P1 4-
C ST [4]-      C U 1-
CA OON 1-      CA OME 2-
CT Y 1-        D BS 1-
D LC [1]-      I EN [1]-
KY U [1]-      IA AS 1-
MD BJ 1-       M CM 1-
MN U 5-        MI U [1]
N IC 1-        MO KL 1-
N NE 1-        N NE 1-
```

REVUE DE PARIS.
SEE -- PARIZER TSAYTSHRIFT.

REVUE DE PHYSIQUE. [ACADEMIA REPUBLICII POPULARE ROMINE] BUCHAREST. 1, 1956-
SUPERSEDES IN PART REVUE DE MATHEMATIQUES ET DE PHYSIQUE. TEXT IN ENGLISH, FRENCH OR GERMAN.

530
```
C U 1-         CA OON 1-
D BS 2-        D LC 1-
D NRL 4-       I ARG 1-
M CM 1-        I CJ 1-
I U 1-         IA AS 1-
IN U 1-        K U 2-
KY U 2-        L U 1-
M CM 1[2]      M H 3-
MI U 1-        MN U 1-
MO KL 1-       N N 1-
N NBELL 1-     N NC 1-
R PB 1-        T ONS 2-
```

REVUE DE PSYCHOLOGIE APPLIQUEE. [CENTRE DE PSYCHOLOGIE APPLIQUEE] PARIS. 1, OC 1950-

150
```
C LU 1-        C U 1-
D AFM 1-       D LC 4-
F MU 7-        F TASU 5-
F U 4-         I CJ 1-
IA U 1-        IN LP 1-
L U 1-         M H [1-5]
M H-M 9-       MD BJ 1-
MI DW 2-3,5-   MI U 1-
MO SU 1-       N IC 1-
N N 1-         N NC 1[2]3
O U 9-         N JR 6-
```

REVUE DE PSYCHOLOGIE DIAGNOSTIQUE ET D'ETUDE DE LA PERSONNALITE.
SEE -- ZEITSCHRIFT FUER DIAGNOSTISCHE PSYCHOLOGIE UND PERSOENLICHKEITSFOR- SCHUNG. REVUE DE PSYCHOLOGIE DIAGNO- STIQUE ET D'ETUDE DE LA PERSONNALITE. REVIEW OF DIAGNOSTIC PSYCHOLOGY AND PERSONALITY EXPLORATION.

REVUE DE QUMRAN. PARIS. 1, JL 1958-
221
```
C BPAC 1-      C LGA 1-
C LSU 1-       C U 1-
C SAT 1-
```

REVUE DE THERAPEUTIQUE MODERNE.
SEE -- MODERN TEDAVI MECMUASI. REVUE DE THERAPEUTIQUE MODERNE.

617.6
REVUE DENTAIRE LIBANAISE. LEBANESE DENTAL MAGAZINE. [ORDRE DU CORPS DENTAIRE DU LIBAN] BEIRUT. 1, 1951-
TEXT IN ENGLISH, FRENCH OR ARABIC. ARABIC SECTION HAS SPECIAL TITLE PAGE.
```
D AFM 1-       G EU [3],10-
P PIU-H [4-6]-
```

382
REVUE DES AGENTS DU COMMERCE EXTERIEUR. [ASSOCIATION NATIONALE DES AGENTS BREVETES DU COMMERCE EXTERIEUR] PARIS.
```
D A [2]-
```

666
REVUE DES AGGLOMERES DE CIMENT. TIJDSCHRIFT DER AGGLOMERATEN MET CEMENT. [CHAMBRE SYNDICALE DES AGGLOMERES DE CIMENT] BRUSSELS.
FRENCH AND/OR FLEMISH.
```
N N [1954]-
```

700
REVUE DES ARTS. [CONSEIL DES MUSEES NATIONAUX] PARIS. 1, 1951- QUARTERLY.
SUPERSEDES MUSEES DE FRANCE.
```
C LU 1-        C U 1-
CT Y 7-        D LC [1]-[3]
D DO 1-        D SI-F 7-     I CA-R 1-
I CU 1-        I U 1-
K YU 1-        KY U 9-
M BU 8-        M H 1-
M NS 1-        M U 1-3
M WELC 1-      MD BJ 1-
M EM 8-        MI U 1-
MO SR 1-       MO SU 4[5]
MO U 1-        N B 9-
N N 1-         N NC 1-
N NOCI 3-      N NMM 1-
NC U 1-        NH D 1-
O CLMA 1-      O U 1-
R PB 1-
```

331.8
REVUE DES CADRES DES INDUSTRIES RADIO-ELECTRIQUES ET ELECTRONIQUES. PARIS.
```
C U 20-
```

FIGURE 30. NEW SERIAL TITLES

Canada. In addition there are literally hundreds of specialized union lists of serials,[10] many of which may cover libraries and serials not found in the larger lists.

In 1961 over 200 published union catalogs and lists were noted by Brummel and Egger in their guide to union catalogs.[11] Some of these are combined records of the books of related libraries, such as the libraries of one county or city. Others are combined lists of special materials, such as scientific periodicals or early printed books. It is by means of a network of such union catalogs and lists and of the published catalogs of a growing number of libraries that the scholar today, although he may lack the convenience of a world-wide library catalog, is able to gain at least partial access to the collections of the libraries of the world.

SUGGESTIONS FOR FURTHER INVESTIGATION

I. Identify a published library catalog which pertains to your field of interest. (See the following list for suggestions.) How could this catalog be useful to you?

Some Library Catalogs in Book Form
    General Libraries
        Bibliothèque Nationale (in progress)
        British Museum
        University of California, Berkeley
        University of California, Los Angeles
    Special Libraries and Collections
        Anthropology
            Bernice P. Bishop Museum Library
            Folklore and Folksong Collection, Cleveland Public Library
            Peabody Museum of Archaeology and Ethnology
        Area Studies
            African Studies
                African Collection, Northwestern University
                African Government Documents Collection, Boston University
                Oriental and African Studies Collection, University of London

[10]For a list of these see U.S. Library of Congress, General Reference and Bibliography Division, *Union Lists of Serials: A Bibliography*, prepared by Ruth A. Freitag (Washington: Library of Congress, 1964).

[11]Leendert Brummel and E. Egger, *Guide to Union Catalogs and International Loan Centers* (The Hague: Martinus Nijhoff, 1961).

Latin American Studies
    Canning House Library, The Hispanic Council—the
        Luso-Brazilian Council, London
    Hispanic Society of America
    Panama Collection, Canal Zone Library—Museum
Oriental Studies
    Oriental and African Studies Collection, University of
        London
    Oriental Collection, New York Public Library
Slavic Studies
    Slavonic Collection, New York Public Library
Business and Economics
    Institute for World Economics, Kiel
    Insurance Library of the Insurance Society of New York
Education
    Collection on Education in Tropical Areas, Institute of
        Education, University of London
Fine Arts
    Avery Architecture Library, Columbia University
    Institute for the Study of Art, Florence
    Metropolitan Museum of Art, New York
    Music Collection, New York Public Library
    Theatre and Drama Collection, New York Public Library
Geography
    American Geographical Society, *Research Catalogue*
Health and Medicine
    London School of Hygiene and Tropical Medicine
    New York Academy of Medicine
History
    Ayer Collection, Americana and American Indians,
       Newberry Library
    Bancroft Library, University of California, Berkeley
    Great Britain. Colonial Office Library
    Great Britain. India Office Library
    Institute for Modern History, Munich
    Mariners' Museum Library, Newport News, Virginia
    U.S. Department of the Interior Library
    Warburg Institute Library
    Western Americana Collection, Yale University
    World War I Collection, New York Public Library
Jewish Culture
    Hebrew Union College—Jewish Institute of Religion Library
    Jewish Collection, New York Public Library

Literature
Defoe Collection, Boston Public Library
Negroes
Schomburg Collection, New York Public Library
Science and Technology
Automotive History Collection, Detroit Public Library
Engineering Societies Library, New York
History of Chemistry Collection, University of Pennsylvania
Horticultural Society Library, Boston
John Crerar Library
Yale Forestry Library
Zoology and Ornithology Library, McGill University
Miscellaneous
American Foundation for the Blind Library
American Numismatic Society Library
Chess Collection, Cleveland Public Library
History of Printing Collection, Newberry Library
Lauriston Castle Chapbooks, National Library of Scotland
Manuscript Collection, New York Public Library
Polar Regions Collection, Dartmouth College

II. Identify and assess the usefulness to you of one or more of the following:
A. A union list of newspapers
B. A union list of manuscripts
C. A union list of serials for British libraries
D. A union list of serials for your state or region
E. A union catalog or list appropriate to your field of interest
F. A union list of serial publications of the United States government.

References for the preceding problems

Brummel, Leendert and E. Egger, *Guide to Union Catalogs and Inter-national Loan Centers.* The Hague: Martinus Nijhoff, 1961.

U.S. Library of Congress, General Reference and Bibliography Division, *Union Lists of Serials: A Bibliography,* prepared by Ruth A. Freitag. Washington: Library of Congress, 1964.

Malclès, Louise-Noëlle, *Les Sources du Travail Bibliographique.* Genève: E. Droz; Lille: Giard, 1950–58, 4 vols.

Winchell, Constance M. *Guide to Reference Books.* 8th ed. Chicago: American Library Association, 1967; *First Supplement, 1965–1966.* Chicago: American Library Association, 1968.

VI

SUBJECT BIBLIOGRAPHY

How index-learning turns no student pale,
Yet holds the eel of science by the tail.

—*Alexander Pope*[1]

Of all forms of the orderly presentation of records perhaps the most complex is that of subject bibliography. The term refers to lists which are limited to one or more subjects, or which are arranged primarily by subject.

SUBJECT LISTS

As long as the scholar was able to know and remember the names of all persons working and writing in his field, the author bibliography sufficed. But as knowledge grew and became fragmented into specialties the need arose to assemble works by their subject content. The critical point seems to have been reached in the nineteenth century, if one may judge from the number of great bibliographies produced. More or less typical is that by James C. Pilling, who brought together from government offices, mission libraries, and the libraries of private citizens over 4,000 titles concerned with North American Indian languages.[2] He regarded his list as a tentative one and printed only enough copies to be distributed to his collaborators. Later it formed the basis for a series of lists each devoted to an individual language. The page from this work shown in Figure 31 displays titles related to the Coquille, Cheyenne, Ottawa, and Ojibwa languages. The list

---

[1]*The Dunciad*, Book I, line 279.
    [2]James C. Pilling, *Proofsheets of a Bibliography of the Languages of the North American Indians*, Bureau of American Ethnology, Miscellaneous Publications no. 2 (Washington: Government Printing Office, 1885).

BIBLIOGRAPHY

OF THE

LANGUAGES OF THE NORTH AMERICAN INDIANS.

By James C. Pilling.

1 **Abbott** (G. H.) Vocabulary of the Coquille.
Manuscript. 3 ll. folio. In the library of the Bureau of Ethnology. Collected in 1858 at the Siletz Indian Agency.

2 **Abert** (*Lieut.* James William). 30th Congress 1st Session. (Senate.) Executive, No. 23. | Report | of | the Secretary of War, | communicating | in | Answer to a resolution of the Senate, a report and map of the ex- | amination of New-Mexico, made by Lieutenant J. W. Abert, of | the topographical corps. | **BA. LSH.**
[No title page. Letter of the Secretary of War dated Feb. 4, 1848. Lieut. Abert's letter same date.]
Pp. 1–132. 8°. map.
Numerals (1–100) of the Cheyenne, p. 11. Vocabulary of the Cheyenne, pp. 12–14. This report reprinted as follows:

3 —— Report of Lieut. J. W. Abert, of his examination of New Mexico, in the years 1846–'47.
In **Emory** (W. H.) Notes of a Military Reconnoissance, pp. 417–548. Washington, 1848. 8°.
Numerals and vocabulary of the Cheyenne, pp. 427, 428–430.
The vocabulary reprinted in **Gallatin** (A.) Hale's Indians of N. W. America, in **Am. Eth. Soc.** Trans., vol. 2, p. cxiv.

4 **Abinodjiiag** | Omasinaiganiwan. |
Buffalo: | Press of Oliver G. Steele. | 1837. | **BA.**
Pp. 1–8. 18°. First lessons in the Ottawa language. Reprinted as follows:

5 **Abinodjiiag** | Omassinaiganiwan. |
Detroit: | Bogg & Harmon, Printers. | 1845. | **BA.**
Pp. 1–8. 18°.

6 **Abinoji** | aki tibajimouin. | In the Ojibwa language. |
Boston: | Printed for the American Board of Commissioners | for Foreign Missions, by Crocker & Brewster. | 1840. | **ABC. BA. HU.**
Pp. 1–139. 12°. Geography for beginners; taken principally from the Peter Parley series.

1

is arranged by authors, with an index of languages and dialects at the end of the volume. Libraries where copies of some of these titles are available are indicated by the symbols near the right-hand margin. Such a bibliography has obvious value for the scholar. If his subject were the Coquille language, for example, he need no longer travel to obscure mission libraries in search of material. By means of subject bibliographies such as Pilling's, much drudgery has been eliminated from scholarship and many important titles have been saved from oblivion.

INDEXES TO PERIODICALS

At about the same time that Pilling was compiling his list another bibliographic development was taking place as a result of the growing popularity of the periodical, which had begun to rival the book as a source of information. The relatively short periodical article, buried among miscellaneous and unrelated matter, was difficult to identify and locate. One of the first persons to attack this problem on a broad scale was William Frederick Poole. While a student at Yale College in the mid-nineteenth century, he began a subject index to whatever periodicals were at hand as an aid to his fellow students in preparing their essays and debates. As he put it, "My work, though crude and feeble on its bibliographic side, answered its purpose, and brought to me the whole body of students for a kind of help they they could not get from library catalogues, nor from any other source." As the original manuscript of his index began to wear out, Poole yielded to requests to print it. Later he was urged to revise and update it, which he did in an edition of 1852. Finally he turned the project over to the American Library Association which, with the Library Association in England, brought out *Poole's Index to Periodical Literature* in 1891.[3] With its supplements it forms an index to almost 500 periodicals, covering the years 1802 to 1907.

A page from this index (Figure 32) shows titles in English only, for Poole's includes no foreign language periodicals. The subjects are not, for the most part, highly technical. Poole limited his index to those general and popular journals likely to be available in most libraries. He specifically excluded "medical, legal, botanical, microscopical and other purely professional and scientific serials." This is an index by subjects only.[4] For each

---

[3]*Poole's Index to Periodical Literature,* 1802–1881, rev. ed. (Boston: Houghton, Mifflin and Company, 1891), 2 vols. Supplements 1882–1907 (Boston: Houghton, Mifflin and Company, 1887–1908), 5 vols.

[4]An author index to periodicals of the nineteenth century is the *Wellesley Index to Victorian Periodicals, 1824–1900*, ed: Walter E. Houghton (Toronto: University of Toronto Press, 1966–   ) in progress.

article listed the abbreviated title of the periodical is given, with the volume and page and the author's name if it is known. The date must be determined by consulting a table elsewhere in the volume. As it records these articles of a former era, Poole's index reveals the tastes and interests of that time. In Figure 32, for example, the large number of articles devoted to phrenology attests to the wide popularity that this subject enjoyed. Eyewitness accounts of historical events, reviews of contemporary books, and fashions in thought and dress in the English-speaking world of the nineteenth century have been made more accessible through Poole's index.

It remained to find a means of making equally accessible the articles which were currently being published in a rapidly growing number of periodicals. Beginning with the year 1900 the H.W. Wilson Company began to issue the *Readers' Guide to Periodical Literature*, covering a number of current periodicals.[5] Improvements introduced into this index included author and title entries, standard subject headings, dates and inclusive paging, and cumulations which kept the index up to date without unduly increasing the number of volumes through which the user must search. Today the *Readers' Guide* indexes some 150 periodicals, generally of a popular and non-technical nature, as may be seen from the list in Figure 33. Subjects range from astronomy (*Sky and Telescope*) to boating (*Yachting*) and from photography (*Modern Photography*) to foreign affairs (*Department of State Bulletin*). In this, as in many other Wilson indexes, the selection of periodicals is made with the advice of librarians who are in constant touch with the needs of users.

Like many other inventions of the nineteenth century the periodical index has become a commonplace today. The *Readers' Guide* was followed in 1916 by a supplement which grew to become the *Social Sciences and Humanities Index*.[6] Based on the same general principles, it covered periodicals which were less popular and more scholarly (see Figure 34). In 1929 still another index appeared, the *Education Index*, which undertook to cover selected periodicals dealing with schools and teaching.[7] (See Figure 34 also.) Other specialized periodical indexes followed. A list of some of these, illustrating their variety, is at the end of this chapter.

---

[5]*Readers' Guide to Periodical Literature*, 1900–date (New York: The H.W. Wilson Co., 1905–date), semimonthly with cumulations.

[6]*Social Sciences and Humanities Index*, 1916–date (New York: The H.W. Wilson Co., 1905–date), quarterly with cumulations.

[7]*Education Index*, 1929–date (New York: The H.W. Wilson Co., 1932–date), monthly with cumulations.

Photography; New Action of Light. (M. Niepce de St. Victor) J. Frankl. Inst. 65: 336.
— New Chapter in. Once a Week, 6: 688.
— New Processes of. Pop. Sci. Mo. 13: 441.
— New Uses of. All the Year, 41: 89.
— of southern Star-Clusters. (C. S. Sellack) Am. J. Sci. 106: 15.
— on Glass, 1851. J. Frankl. Inst. 53: 120.
— on Paper and on Glass. Art J. 2: 261.
— Origin and Progress of. Nat. M. 1: 510.
— Paper Negatives in. (L. Warnerke) J. Frankl. Inst. 100: 67.
— Phosphorescence and Fluorescence shown by. (M. Niepce de St. Victor) J. Frankl. Inst. 65: 50.
— Physics in. (W. de W. Abney) Nature, 18: 489–543.
— Practical. (J. Sidebotham) Recr. Sci. 1: 335.
— Present State of. Nat. R. 8: 365.
— Printing Process. (J. Sidebotham) Recr. Sci. 2: 119.
— Progress of, 1853. Art J. 5: 181. — (Sir D. Brewster) No. Brit. 36: 170. — House. Words, 9: 242. Same art. Ecl. M. 32: 506.
— Recent Discoveries in. (J. T. Taylor) Pop. Sci. R. 14: 395.
— Researches in. (R. Meldola) Nature, 10: 281. Same art. Pop. Sci. Mo. 5: 717.
— Sensitiveness of Silver Bromide to. Pract. M. 3: 47.
— Supposed Discovery of, by Boulton, 1790. (T. Coryton) Fortn. 20: 64. Same art. Liv. Age, 118: 346. Same art. Ecl. M. 81: 363.
— a suppressed Art. (J. Carpenter) Once a Week, 10: 368.
— Tissandier's. (R. Meldola) Nature, 13: 204.
— Theory of. (H. Vogel) J. Frankl. Inst. 77: 122, 182.
— Waterglass in. (T. A. Malone) Recr. Sci. 1: 20.
— ... 10: 484.

Phrenology. (T. Bradford) No. Am. 37: 59. — (T. Flint) Knick. 2: 103. — (C. Ticknor) Knick. 13: 308. — (L. A. Atwater) Chr. Q. Spec. 7: 274. — (J. D. Whelpley) Am. Whig R. 3: 32. — Am. J. Sci. 39: 65. — Am. Q. 20: 366. — So. R. 6: 265. — So. Lit. J. 1: 393. 2: 479. — (J. Moultrie) So. Lit. J. 3: 1. — For. Q. 2: 1. — Brit. & For. R. 12: 142. — Ed. Mo. R. 3: 123. — (A. B. Dod) Princ. 10: 279. — Lit. & Theo. R. 5: 641. — Brit. Q. 4: 397. Same art. Ecl. M. 10: 188. — For. R. 4: 263. — New Eng. M. 6: 467. 8: 182. — Blackw. 11: 35, 365. 10: 73, 682. 13: 100, 199. — Ed. R. 2: 147. 25: 227. 45: 248. — Mo. R. 94: 395. 118: 534. — Colburn, 10: 533. — Lond. M. 15: 453. — Portfo.(Den.) 27: 353. — (D. Uwins) Colburn, 34: 445. — Am. Mo. M. 11: 354. — West. Mo. R. 1: 357. — Am. Mo. M. 4: 9. — (E. Pond) Bib. Sac. 10: 641. 11: 19. — Dub. Univ. 64: 158. — Lond. M. 8: 541. — West. M. 1: 133, 200.
— and Mr. George Combe. Fraser, 22: 509.
— and Fact. (J. T. Peck) Meth. Q. 7: 557.
— and its Opponents. Dub. Univ. 3: 570.
— and Power of the Will over Others. (H. S. Thomson) Zoist, 3: 319.
— and Psychology. (A. Bain) Fraser, 61: 692.
— and Revelation. (D. W. Clark) Meth. Q. 7: 165. — Chr. R. 1: 348.
— applied to Painting and Sculpture. (J. W. Jackson) Zoist, 13: 406.
— as it affects Free-Will. Zoist, 3: 416.
— Brain of Manning, the Murderer. (J. Elliotson) Zoist, 9: 335.
— Caldwell's Elements of. West. Mo. R. 1: 465.
— Carpenter's Views of. (T. S. Prideaux) Zoist, 4: 480.
— Cerebral Development. (J. Straton) Zoist, 6: 291. — ... 8: 396.

FIGURE 32. POOLE'S INDEX TO PERIODICAL LITERATURE [*Poole's Index to Periodical Literature*, 1802–81, vol. 1, Part 2, p. 1004, (1802–81). Used by permission of the Peter Smith Co. and the Houghton Mifflin Company.]

ABBREVIATIONS OF PERIODICALS INDEXED

March 1966—February 1967

FOR FULL INFORMATION, CONSULT PAGES IX–XI

ALA Bul—ALA Bulletin
Am Artist—American Artist
Am City—American City
Am Ed—American Education
Am For—American Forests
*Am Heritage—American Heritage
Am Hist R—American Historical Review
Am Home—American Home
Am Rec G—American Record Guide
America—America
Américas—Américas
Ann Am Acad—Annals of the American Acad
emy of Political and Social Science
Antiques—Antiques
Arch Forum—Architectural Forum
Arch Rec—Architectural Record
Art N—Art News
*Atlan—Atlantic
Audubon—Audubon
Aviation W—Aviation Week & Space Tech-
nology

Bet Hom & Gard—Better Homes and Gardens
Bsns W—Business Week
Bul Atomic Sci—Bulletin of the Atomic Sci-
entists

Cath World—Catholic World
*Changing T—Changing Times
Christian Cent—Christian Century
Commentary—Commentary
Commonweal—Commonweal
Cong Digest—Congressional Digest
*Consumer Bul—Consumer Bulletin
Consumer Rep—Consumer Reports
Craft Horiz—Craft Horizons
Cur Hist—Current History

Dance Mag—Dance Magazine
Dept State Bul—Department of State Bulletin
Design—Design
Duns R—Dun's Review
Formerly Dun's Review and Modern
Industry

Ebony—Ebony
Electr World—Electronics World
Esquire—Esquire

*Farm J—Farm Journal (Central edition)
Field & S—Field & Stream
Flower Grower—Flower Grower, The Home
Garden
Continued as Home Garden & Flower
Grower Feb '67
Flying—Flying
Focus—Focus
*For Affairs—Foreign Affairs
Fortune—Fortune

*Good H—Good Housekeeping

*Harper—Harper's Magazine
Harvard Bsns R—Harvard Business Review
*Hi Fi—High Fidelity incorporating Musical
America
Hobbies—Hobbies
*Holiday—Holiday
Home Gard—Home Garden & Flower Grower
*Horizon—Horizon
Horn Bk—Horn Book Magazine
Horticulture—Horticulture
Hot Rod—Hot Rod
House & Gard—House & Garden incorporating
Living for Young Homemakers
House B—House Beautiful

Int Concil—International Conciliation

*Ladies Home J—Ladies' Home Journal
Library J—Library Journal
Life—Life
Liv Wildn—Living Wilderness
*Look—Look (Middle Atlantic edition)

McCalls—McCall's
Miss & Roc—Missiles and Rockets
Continued as Technology Week Je 6 '66
Mlle—Mademoiselle
Mo Labor R—Monthly Labor Review
Mod Phot—Modern Photography
Motor B—Motor Boating
Motor T—Motor Trend

NEA J—NEA Journal
N Y Times Mag—New York Times Magazine
*Nat Geog Mag—National Geographic Magazine
Nat Parks Mag—National Parks Magazine
Nat R—National Review (44p issue only, pub.
in alternate weeks)
Nation—Nation
Nations Bsns—Nation's Business
*Natur Hist—Natural History incorporating
Nature Magazine
Negro Hist Bul—Negro History Bulletin
New Repub—New Republic
New Yorker—New Yorker
*Newsweek—Newsweek

Opera N—Opera News
Outdoor Life—Outdoor Life

PTA Mag—PTA Magazine
Parents Mag—Parents' Magazine and Better
Homemaking
Parks & Rec—Parks & Recreation
Plays—Plays
Poetry—Poetry
Pop Electr—Popular Electronics
Pop Gard—Popular Gardening & Living Out-
doors
Pop Mech—Popular Mechanics
Pop Phot—Popular Photography
Pop Sci—Popular Science Monthly
Pub W—Publishers' Weekly

*Read Digest—Reader's Digest (Great Lakes
edition)
Redbook—Redbook
Reporter—The Reporter

Sat Eve Post—Saturday Evening Post
Sat R—Saturday Review
Sch & Soc—School and Society
Sch Arts—School Arts
Sci Am—Scientific American
Sci Digest—Science Digest
Sci N—Science News
Formerly Science News Letter
Sci N L—Science News Letter
Continued as Science News Mr 12 '66
Science—Science
*Seventeen—Seventeen
Sky & Tel—Sky and Telescope
*Sports Illus—Sports Illustrated
Sr Schol—Senior Scholastic (Teacher edition)
Suc Farm—Successful Farming (Eastern edi-
tion)
Sunset—Sunset (Central edition)

Tech W—Technology Week including Missiles
and Rockets
Formerly Missiles and Rockets
Time—Time
Todays Health—Today's Health
Travel—Travel

UN Mo Chron—UN Monthly Chronicle
UNESCO Courier—UNESCO Courier
U S Camera—U.S. Camera & Travel
U S News—U.S. News & World Report

Vital Speeches—Vital Speeches of the Day
Vogue—Vogue

Wilson Lib Bul—Wilson Library Bulletin
*Writer—Writer

Yachting—Yachting
Yale R—Yale Review

* Available for blind and other physically handicapped readers on talking books, in braille,
or on magnetic tape. For information address Division for the Blind and Physically Handicapped,
Library of Congress, Washington, D.C. 20542

FIGURE 33. PERIODICALS INDEXED BY THE READERS' GUIDE TO PERIODICAL LITERA-
TURE [Readers' Guide to Periodical Literature, vol. 26, (March, 1966–February,
1967). Used by permission of the H. W. Wilson Company.]

ABBREVIATIONS OF PUBLICATIONS INDEXED

JULY 1966—JUNE 1967

For full information consult pages vii-xii

AAUP Bul—AAUP Bulletin
ALA Bul—ALA Bulletin
AV Comm R—AV Communication Review
AV Instr—Audiovisual Instruction
Adult Ed—Adult Education
Adult Lead—Adult Leadership
Ag Ed Mag—The Agricultural Education Magazine
Am Ann Deaf—American Annals of the Deaf
Am Assn Col Teach Ed Yrbk—American Association of Colleges for Teacher Education. Yearbook
Am Assn Health Phys Ed Rec Res Q—American Association for Health, Physical Education, and Recreation. Research Quarterly
Am Assn Sch Adm Official Report—American Association of School Administrators. Official Report
Am Biol Teach—The American Biology Teacher
Am Council Ind Arts Teach Ed Yrbk—American Council on Industrial Arts Teacher Education. Yearbook
Am Ed—American Education
Am J Men Deficiency—American Journal of Mental Deficiency (Monograph Supplements included)
Am Mus Teach—The American Music Teacher
Am Sch & Univ—American School & University
Am Sch Bd J—The American School Board Journal
Am Voc J—American Vocational Journal
Arith Teach—The Arithmetic Teacher
Ariz Teach—Arizona Teacher
Art Ed—Art Education
Arts & Activities—Arts and Activities
Assn Sch Bsns Officials U S & Canada Proc—Association of School Business Officials of the United States and Canada. Proceedings
Assn Stud Teach Yrbk—Association for Student

Ed—Education
Ed & Psychol M—Educational and Psychological Measurement
Ed Digest—The Education Digest
Ed Forum—The Educational Forum
Ed Lead—Educational Leadership
Ed Rec—The Educational Record
Ed Rec Bur Bul—Educational Records Bureau. Bulletins
Ed Res—Educational Research (British)
Ed Screen AV G—Educational Screen AV Guide
Ed Theatre J—Educational Theatre Journal
Ed Theory—Educational Theory
El Engl—Elementary English
El Sch J—The Elementary School Journal
Engl J—English Journal
Engl Lang Teach—English Language Teaching
Excep Child—Exceptional Children

Forecast Home Econ—Forecast for Home Economics
Formerly Practical Forecast for Home Economics
French R—The French Review

German Q—The German Quarterly
Grade Teach—Grade Teacher

ABBREVIATIONS OF PERIODICALS INDEXED

For full information see pages vii-x

Acad Pol Sci Proc—Academy of Political Science. Proceedings
Afric Affairs—African Affairs
Africa R—Africa Report
Am Anthrop—American Anthropologist
Am Antiq—American Antiquity
Am Behav Sci—American Behavioral Scientist
Am Econ R—American Economic Review
Am Econ R Pa & Proc—American Economic Review; Papers and Proceedings
Am J Archaeol—American Journal of Archaeology
Am J Econ—American Journal of Economics and Sociology
Am J Int Law—American Journal of International Law
Am J Philol—American Journal of Philology
Am J Sociol—American Journal of Sociology
Am Lit—American Literature
Am Orient Soc J—American Oriental Society Journal
Am Pol Sci R—American Political Science Review
Am Q—American Quarterly
Am Sch Orient Res Bul—American Schools of Oriental Research. Bulletin
Am Scholar—American Scholar
Am Sociol R—American Sociological Review
Am Speech—American Speech
Am West—American West
Americas—Americas
Antioch R—Antioch Review
Arion—Arion
Asian S—Asian Survey
Assn Am Geog Ann—Association of American Geographers. Annals
Com Q—Atlantic Com... Quarterly

Encounter—Encounter
Engl Hist R—English Historical Review
Engl Stud—English Studies
Essays Crit—Essays in Criticism
Ethics—Ethics
Ethnology—Ethnology

Geog J—Geographical Journal
Geog R—Geographical Review
Germ R—Germanic Review

Harv J Asiatic Stud—Harvard Journal of Asiatic Studies
Harv R—Harvard Review
Harv Theol R—Harvard Theological Review
Hispan Am Hist R—Hispanic American Historical Review
Hispan R—Hispanic Review
Hist & Theory—History & Theory
Hist Today—History Today
Historian—Historian
History—History
Hudson R—Hudson Review
Human Organ—Human Organization
Human Relations—Human Relations

Int Affairs—International Affairs
Int J Am Ling—International Journal of American Linguistics
Int J Comp Sociol—International Journal of Comparative Sociology
ah R—Internati...

FIGURE 34. PERIODICALS INDEXED BY THE SOCIAL SCIENCES AND HUMANITIES INDEX (LEFT) AND THE EDUCATION INDEX (RIGHT) [*Social Sciences and Humanities Index*, vol. 20 (April, 1966-March, 1967); and *The Education Index*, vol. 17 (July, 1966–June, 1967). Used by permission of The H. W. Wilson Company.]

AN INDEX TO ESSAYS

An index that does for the essay and for the chapter in a book what the *Readers' Guide* does for the periodical article is the *Essay and General Literature Index.*[8] In Figure 35 a page from this work shows entries by author (Padgett), subject (Pacificism), and title (*The Pagan School*), with subjects ranging from packinghouse workers to paleontology, and including such a relatively elusive topic as paganism in literature. The author and title of the essay are given, followed by the author and title of the book in which it occurs, and the numbers of the pages which it covers. For example, an essay about Vance Packard's *The Status Seekers*, written by C. Cruise O'Brien and entitled "Free Spenders," occurs in Cruise O'Brien's book *Writers and Politics*, on pages 23 to 27. A bibliographic description of the latter title is found in a list of books indexed, located at the end of the volume.

TYPES OF SUBJECT INDEX

The Alphabetical Index

The Essay and General Literature Index, like traditional subject bibliography generally, uses words and phrases as subject headings, and arranges them in alphabetical order. The use of such indexes is sometimes complicated by the difficulty of selecting from several synonymous terms one word or phrase to designate a subject. (See, in Figure 35, *Paleolithic period*. In this case there is a cross-reference to *Stone age.*) Other problems revolve around the use of inverted headings (see *Painting, American*, but *Pakistan literature*), or subdivisions of a subject (see *Paleontology—Devonian*). With a complex subject such as wheat prices in Canada, one must choose among the terms *wheat, prices,* and *Canada*. One may wonder, in using an alphabetical subject index, whether to approach the subject *bees* through the more general topic *insects.* Finally, the alphabetic arrangement tends to obscure logical relationships between subjects and to separate related topics. Books about Defoe, in the alphabetical index, follow books about Chaucer not because of any relationship between the work of the two writers, but because *D* follows *C*.

---

[8]*Essay and General Literature Index*, 1900–date (New York: The H.W. Wilson Co., 1934–date), semi-annual with cumulations.

Pacey, Desmond—*Continued*
The writer and his public: 1920-1960
In Klinck, C. F. ed. Literary history of Canada p477-95
Pacific settlement of international disputes.
See Arbitration, International
Pacifici, Sergio
Italian novels of the fifties
In Kostelanetz, R. ed. On contemporary literature p159-73
Something old and something new
In Kostelanetz, R. ed. On contemporary literature p174-79
Pacifism
James, W. The moral equivalent of war; excerpt from "Memories and studies"
In Bramson, L. and Goethals, G. W. eds. War: studies from psychology, sociology, anthropology p21-31
Packard, Sidney Raymond
A medievalist looks at the Renaissance
In The Renaissance reconsidered p3-12
Packard, Vance Oakley
About individual works
The status seekers
Cruise O'Brien, C. Free spenders
In Cruise O'Brien, C. Writers and politics p23-27
Packing-house workers
East St Louis
Purcell, T. V. The hopes of Negro workers for their children
In Shostak, A. B. and Gomberg, W. eds. Blue-collar world p144-54
Kansas City
Purcell, T. V. The hopes of Negro workers for their children
In Shostak, A. B. and Gomberg, W. eds. Blue-collar world p144-54
Paden, William D.
Tennyson's The lover's tale, R. H. Shepherd, and T. J. Wise
In Virginia. University. Bibliographical Society. Studies in bibliography v18 p111-45
Padgett, Leon Vincent
Mexico's one-party system: a re-evaluation
In Martz, J. D. ed. The dynamics of change in Latin American politics p223-27
Padua. Università
Woodward, W. H. Vittorino da Feltre
In Woodward, W. H. Vittorino da Feltre and other humanist educators p 1-92
The pagan school. Baudelaire, C. P.
In Baudelaire, C. P. Baudelaire, as a literary critic p72-77
Paganism
Lewis, C. S. Selected materials: the seminal period
In Lewis, C. S. The discarded image p45-91
Paganism in literature
Lewis, C. S. Selected materials: the seminal period
In Lewis, C. S. The discarded image p45-91
Pain. See Suffering

Paine, Thomas
The age of reason; excerpt from "The complete writings of Thomas Paine"
In Ekirch, A. A. ed. Voices in dissent p22-29
About
Browne, R. B. The Paine-Burke controversy in eighteenth-century Irish popular songs
In Browne, R. B.; Roscelli, W. J. and Loftus, R. J. eds. The Celtic cross p80-97
Painter, Gamaliel
About
Lee, W. S. The vision of a Yankee: Middlebury, Vermont
In Wheeler, T. C. ed. A vanishing America p15-33
Painters, Italian
Sartre, J. P. The prisoner of Venice
In Sartre, J. P. Situations p 1-60
Painters, Women. See Artists, Women
Painting
Kandinskiï, V. V. Reminiscences
In Herbert, R. L. ed. Modern artists on art p19-44
See also Expressionism (Art)
Venice
Sartre, J. P. The prisoner of Venice
In Sartre, J. P. Situations p 1-60
Painting, American
Kozloff, M. The new American painting
In Kostelanetz, R. ed. The new American arts p88-116
Painting, French
White, C. and White, H. Institutional change in the French painting world
In Wilson, R. N. ed. The arts in society p255-70
Paintings, Abstract. See Art, Abstract
Paintings, Non-objective. See Art, Abstract
Pakistan literature
20th century—History and criticism
Gauhar, A. Urdu literature in Pakistan: the writer's problem
In International Federation of Modern Languages and Literature. Literary history & literary criticism p194-203
Paleolithic period. See Stone age
Paleontology
Haury, E. W. The first Americans
In Gabel, C. ed. Man before history p36-39
Devonian
Stevens, M. S. Thoracic armor of a new arthrodire (holonema) from the Devonian of Presque Isle County, Michigan
In Michigan Academy of Science, Arts and Letters. Papers, v49 p163-75
Mississippian
Dorr, J. A. and Moser, F. Ctenacanth sharks from the mid-Mississippian of Michigan
In Michigan Academy of Science, Arts and Letters. Papers, v49 p105-13

FIGURE 35.   ESSAY AND GENERAL LITERATURE INDEX (*Essay and General Literature Index*, 1965, p. 206. Used by permission of the H. W. Wilson Company.)

The Classified Index

A type of index which manages to avoid some of the problems presented by the alphabetical arrangement is illustrated by the *Index of Economic Journals*.[9] This is a *classified index*, which presents its subjects in logical relation to each other by means of a system of classification. In this index (Figure 36) it is necessary, in order to find an article on the elasticity of demand, first to locate the topic in a classification schedule, where it appears at 2.114. At this point in the body of the index (Figure 37) are listed four articles concerning elasticity of demand. The user of this index does not have to choose between the headings *demand* and *elasticity* or to select a synonymous term. Furthermore he finds his topic among related subjects such as *demand analysis* and *rationing*. He must, however, understand the relationship of his topic to the larger body of knowledge in order to find it in the classification schedule. (In the *Index of Economic Journals* he will be aided by an alphabetical subject index as well as an author index included in each volume.)

The KWIC, or Permuted Title Index

The use of the computer in indexing has given rise to some radically different kinds of index. One of these, the *KWIC (Key Word In Context)* or *permuted title index*, is illustrated in Figure 38.[10] It is produced by listing titles successively by each significant word. By this method great numbers of titles may be arranged quickly, but indexing is limited to words which appear in the titles. For example, in Figure 38 the report, "Measurements of Lunar Temperature Variations During an Eclipse and Throughout a Lunation," may be found under the words *lunar, lunation,* and *eclipse,* but would not appear under the word *moon.*

The Citation Index

Another computer-produced index is the *citation index*, exemplified by *Science Citation Index*.[11] The user of this type of index begins with any work which he knows to be relevant to his subject. By finding this work listed in the citation index, he is able to trace subsequent works in which it has been cited. For example, in Figure 39, the article by L. Corrsin,

---

[9]American Economic Association, *Index of Economic Journals* (Homewood, Ill.: Richard D. Irwin, Inc., Vol. I (1886–1924)—date.

[10]U.S. Department of Commerce, Office of Technical Services, *Keywords Index to U.S. Government Technical Reports,* XV (January 15, 1963), pp. A22, A40.

[11]*Science Citation Index* (Philadelphia: Institute for Scientific Information, 1961–date).

CLASSIFICATION SCHEDULE

1. **SCOPE AND METHOD OF ECONOMICS**

    1.0 GENERAL
    1.1 METHODOLOGY

        1.10 General
        1.11 Philosophy
        1.12 Use of Mathematics
            (For mathematical and econometric tools see 7)
        1.13 Empirical Research
        1.14 Historicism. Institutionalism
            (For Historical and Institutionalist Schools see 4.6)
        1.15 Marginalism
            (For marginal cost analysis see 2.123; full cost vs. marginal cost controversy, 2.1334)
        1.16 Catholic Economics
        1.17 Relation of Economics to Other Disciplines
        1.18 Relation of Economics to Policy
            (For economic systems see 3)

    1.2 ROLE OF THE ECONOMIST
    1.3 TEACHING OF ECONOMICS
        (For business education see 14.231; education of agricultural economists, 16.031; teach-
        ing of industrial relations, 19.52; education of city and regional planners, 22.0)
    1.4 RESEARCH. BIBLIOGRAPHY
        (For research and bibliographies on special subjects see subject)
    1.5 ECONOMIC SOCIETIES. PERIODICALS

2. **ECONOMIC THEORY, INCLUDING MONETARY THEORY**
    (For fiscal theory see 10; international trade theory, 11; theory of population, 18.0)

    2.0 GENERAL
        2.01 Motivation
            (For utility maximization see 2.111; profit maximization of the firm, 2.1311)
        2.114 Elasticity of Demand

FIGURE 36. PART OF THE CLASSIFICATION SCHEDULE FOR THE INDEX OF ECONOMIC JOURNALS [*Index of Economic Journals*, vol. I (Homewood, Ill.: Richard D. Irwin, Inc.) p. xxii. Used by permission of the publisher.]

2. ECONOMIC THEORY, ETC.

2.1 VALUE, PRICE, AND ALLOCATION THEORY (Cont.)

2.10 GENERAL (Cont.)

theory of value. QJE 15:321-47 May 01

Taylor, W. G. L. Some important phases in the evolution of the idea of value. JPE 3: 414-33 Sep 95

Usher, A. P. The content of the value concept. QJE 31:711-18 Aug 17

Young, A. A. Some limitations of the value concept. QJE 25:409-28 May 11

2.11 UTILITY. DEMAND. THEORY OF THE HOUSEHOLD

2.110 GENERAL

Furnivall, J. S. The organisation of consumption. EJ 20:23-30 Mar 10

2.111 UTILITY AND INDIFFERENCE ANALYSIS

Chapman, S. J. The utility of income and progressive taxation. EJ 23:25-35 Mar 13

Clark, J. B. A universal law of economic variation. QJE 8:261-79 Apr 94

Clark, J. M. Economics and modern psychology. Pt. I-II. JPE 26:1-30; 136-66 Jan, Feb 18

Cooley, C. H. The progress of pecuniary valuation. QJE 30:1-21 Nov 15

Davenport, H. J. Proposed modifications in Austrian theory and terminology. QJE 16:355-84 May 02

Dickinson, Z. C. The relations of recent psychological developments to economic

2.113 DEMAND ANALYSIS

Hansen, A. H. Certain aspects of demand in relation to the business cycle. AER 14: 13-16 Mar 24

Hardy, C. O. Real demand and market price. AER 14:524-25 Sep 24

Hoxie, R. F. The demand and supply concepts: an introduction to the study of market price. Pt. I-II. JPE 14:337-61; 401-26 Jun, Jul 06

Mitchell, W. C. The backward art of spending money. AER 2:269-81 Jun 12

2.114 ELASTICITY OF DEMAND

Lehfeldt, R. A. The elasticity of demand for wheat. EJ 24:212-17 Jun 14

Moore, H. L. Elasticity of demand and flexibility of prices. JASA 18:8-19 Mar 22

Pigou, A. C. A method of determining the numerical value of elasticities of demand. EJ 20:636-40 Dec 10

Schultz, H. Elasticity of demand and the coefficient of correlation [followed by R. S. Vaile's comment]. QJE 38:169-72 Nov 23

2.115 RATIONING

Bowley, A. L. The theoretical effects of rationing on prices. EJ 30:340-47 Sep 20

Fish, A. L. Dr. MacFarlane on "complementary goods." JPE 8:238-41 Mar 00

Fisher, I. Is "utility" the most suitable term for the concept it is used to denote?

FIGURE 37. INDEX OF ECONOMIC JOURNALS [*Index of Economic Journals*; vol. I (Homewood, Ill.: Richard D. Irwin, Inc.) p. 9. Used by permission of the publisher.]

	OF METEORIC ECHOS AD-286 620(K) $2.60 0187
ECLIPSE	MEASUREMENTS OF LUNAR TEMPERATURE VARIATIONS D
	URING AN ECLIPSE AND THROUGHOUT A LUNATION
	AD-286 471(K) $5.60 0348
ECOLOGY	MILITARY SMALL GROUP PERFORMANCE UNDER ISOLATI
	ON AND STRESS. CRITICAL REVIEW. III. ENVIRONME
	NTAL STRESS AND BEHAVIOR ECOLOGY
	AD-286 516(K) $2.60 0208
ECONOMIC	AN ECONOMIC STUDY OF 1000-MEGAWATT HOMOGENEOUS
	REACTOR ORNL-TM-387(K) $9.10 0832
ECONOMIC	ECONOMIC MODELS FOR INDUSTRIAL WAITING LINE PR
	OBLEMS AD-286 383(K) $3.60 0963
ECONOMY	A LIMIT THEOREM ON THE CORE OF AN ECONOMY
	AD-285 997(K) $2.60 0962
ECTEOLA	EFFECT OF IRRADIATION ON THE NATURE OF DNA AS
	EVIDENCED BY FRACTIONATION ON ECTEOLA
	TID-17010(K) $1.60 1049
EDGE	ICING TESTS OF A 10-FT. DELTA WING OF UNITY AS
	PECT RATIO HAVING LEADING EDGE SEPARATION
	AD-280 896(K) $2.60 0751
EDUCATION	INFORMATION RETRIEVAL SYSTEMS AND EDUCATION
	AD-285 535(K) $1.60 0991
EDUCATION	SIMULATION. A VEHICLE FOR FACILITATING INNOVAT
	ION AND SYSTEM DESIGN IN EDUCATION
	AD-285 882(K) $1.60 0994
EIGENVALUES	LOWER BOUNDS FOR HIGHER EIGENVALUES OF SECOND
	ORDER OPERATORS BY FINITE DIFFERENCE METHODS
	AD-286 398(K) $3.60 1069
EJECTOR	INVESTIGATION OF AN AIR EJECTOR PUMP FOR HIGH
	ALTITUDE SAMPLING SYSTEMS
	TID-16973(K) $5.60 0571
EJECTOR	SMALL SCALE EJECTOR MODELS
	AD-286 139(K) $2.60 0175
ELASTIC	RESEARCH AND DEVELOPMENT ON ADVANCED GRAPHITE
	MAT··· ···LUME II ···ATIONS OF ANISOTROP

	AD-286 575(K) $1.60 0109
LUBRICITY	THE EFFECT OF OXIDATION ON GREASE LUBRICITY
	AD-286 175(K) $1.00 0917
LUMINESCENCE	INVESTIGATING THE LUMINESCENCE ORIGINATING DUR
	ING THE ELECTRIC FULMINATION OF THIN WIRES
	AD-286 190(K) $1.10 0140
LUNAR	BIBLIOGRAPHY OF LUNAR AND PLANETARY RESEARCH,
	1961 AD-285 646(K) $8.10 0059
LUNAR	LUNAR RADIO EMISSION
	AD-286 247(K) $1.10 0047
LUNAR	LUNAR REFLECTION STUDY
	AD-286 277(K) $5.60 0569
LUNAR	MEASUREMENTS OF LUNAR TEMPERATURE VARIATIONS D
	URING AN ECLIPSE AND THROUGHOUT A LUNATION
	AD-286 471(K) $5.60 0348
LUNATION	MEASUREMENTS OF LUNAR TEMPERATURE VARIATIONS D
	URING AN ECLIPSE AND THROUGHOUT A LUNATION
	AD-286 471(K) $5.60 0348
LUNN	MATERIAL - PLASTIC CLAMPS (LUNN COMPANY) - EVA
	LUATION OF AD-285 577(K) $1.60 0517
MA-3	LAUNCH AREA PREPARATION AND CHECKOUT. LOGICAL
	FUNCTION REPORT ON OSTF-1 HUMAN FACTORS - PERS
	ONNEL SUBSYSTEM TEST OBJECTIVES (ATLAS MA-3 EN
	GINE SYSTEM) AD-285 868(K) $4.60 0918
MACHINE	A MACHINE THAT READS
	AD-286 604(K) $1.10 0090
MACHINE	NEWS OF THE ACADEMY OF SCIENCES OF THE USSR, D
	EPARTMENT OF TECHNICAL SCIENCES, MECHANICS AND
	MACHINE BUILDING (SELECTED ARTICELS)
	AD-286 613(K) $3.60 0153
MACHINE	SHORT HANDBOOK OF TECHNOLOGY AND MACHINE BUILD
	ING AD-286 590(K) $10.10 0174
MACHINE-BADED	A MACHINE-BADED DOCUMENT CONTROL SYSTEM
	AD-285 883(K) $1.60 0983
MACHINERY	AUXILIARY MACHINERY NOISE AND VIBRATION MEASUR
	EMENTS ··· ···93 CLASS SS(N)-S

FIGURE 38.   A KWIC OR PERMUTED TITLE INDEX

The Far-Infrared Spectra of Metal–Halide Complexes of Pyridine and Related Ligands

By ROBIN J. H. CLARK AND CHARLES S. WILLIAMS

Received August 24, 1964

Metal–halide complexes of pyridine and certain other nitrogen-donor ligands have been extensively investigated in the 200–700 cm.$^{-1}$ region and assignments of metal–halogen ν(M–X) and metal–ligand ν(M–L) stretching vibrations are made. The relationship of the numbers of ν(M–X) and ν(M–L) vibrations and their frequencies to the stereochemistries of the complexes (MX$_m$L$_n$) is outlined. In particular, it is shown that complexes with tetrahedral and octahedral stereochemistries may be clearly distinguished by their infrared patterns. Nujol mull spectra and solution spectra are essentially the same.

Introduction

Relatively few systematic studies of the far-infrared spectra of metal–halide complexes have been carried out. However, with the appearance of commercial double-beam spectrometers capable of reaching down to at least 200 cm.$^{-1}$, data are beginning to accumulate on metal–chlorine ν(M–Cl), metal–bromine ν(M–Br), and in some cases on metal–iodine ν(M–I) stretching vibrations. The assignments were placed on a firm basis by the initial studies on the t$_2$ stretching vibrations of the MX$_4$$^{n-}$ series of anions (M = Mn, Fe, Co, Ni, Cu, Zn) by Clark and Dunn,[1] Adams, *et al.*,[2] and later by Sabatini and Sacconi.[3]

As a natural extension to this work, we have for several years been studying the far-infrared spectra of complexes of the type MX$_m$L$_n$, where L is a neutral electron-donor ligand. Metal–pyridine complexes are among the most extensive series known, and furthermore they include examples of complexes with the following stereochemistries: tetrahedral (MX$_2$·2py) octahedral (MX$_2$·4py, MX$_2$·3py, and MX$_2$·2py) all of which *cis* and *trans* isomers are known), polymeric octahedral and distorted polymeric octahedral (MX$_2$·2py, both of which contain halogen bridges), and *cis*- and *trans*-planar (MX$_2$·2py). A summary of the relevant X-ray information on metal–pyridine complexes is given in Table I.

All the above types of complexes have been included in the present study, and the relationship between

(1) R. J. H. Clark and T. M. Dunn, *J. Chem. Soc.*, 1198 (1963).
(2) D. M. Adams, J. Chatt, J. M. Davidson, and J. Gerratt, *ibid.*, 2189 (1963).

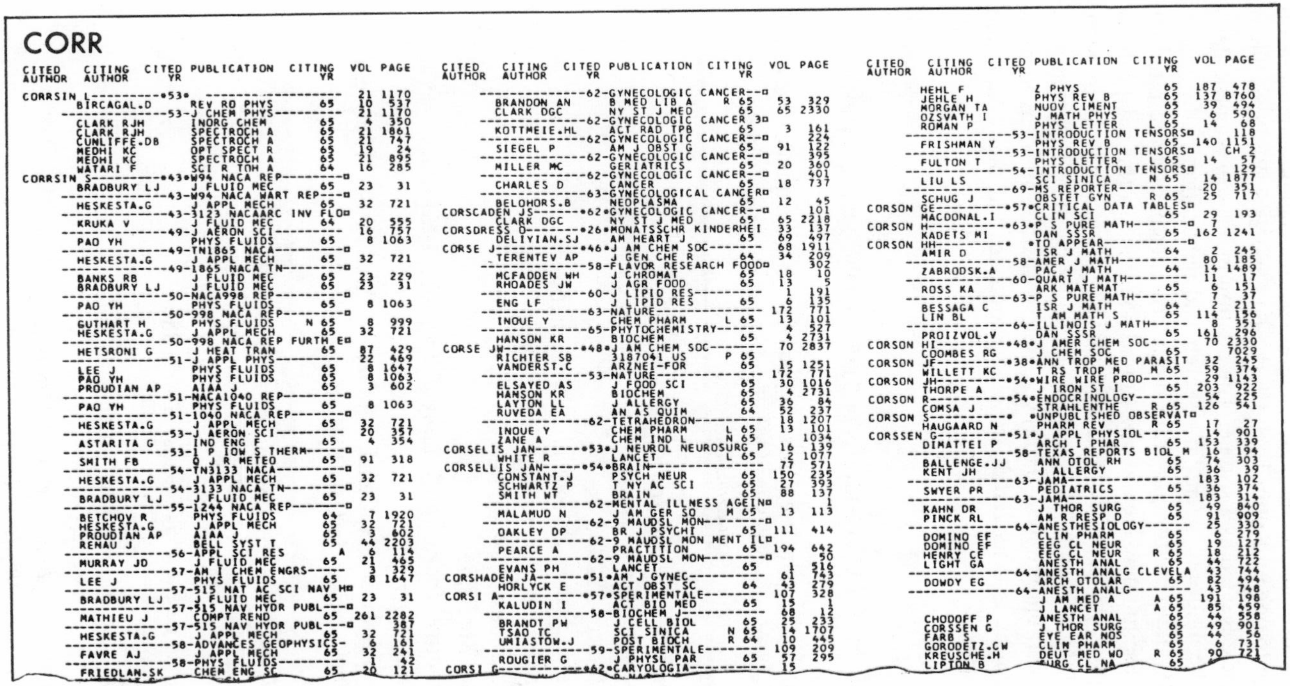

FIGURE 39. SCIENCE CITATION INDEX, WITH A CITING ARTICLE, shown on facing pages. [Reprinted from *Science Citation Index*, 1965 Annual, Part I, columns 3589, 3590, 3591. Copyright 1965 by Institute for Scientific Information; and from *Inorganic Chemistry*, vol. 4, March, 1965, pp. 350, 351. Copyright 1965 by the American Chemical Society. Reprinted by permission of the copyright owners.]

appearing in 1953 in the *Journal of Chemical Physics,* volume 21, page 1170, is known to concern the subject wanted. The citation index leads from this article to one by Robin J. H. Clark and Charles S. Williams where the Corrsin article is cited as a source. The citation index seems particularly well suited to the nature of scientific research and publication.

The KWIC index and the citation index are only two of the attempts being made to use the new technology to find solutions to the old problem of an orderly presentation of records according to their subjects. In some fields, notably that of medicine, literature searching by means of computer has made considerable progress. However, unless or until an ideal form of subject bibliography is discovered, we may expect to find many new and experimental forms.

SUGGESTIONS FOR FURTHER INVESTIGATION

I. Identify and assess the usefulness to you of a periodical index pertinent to your field of interest. See the following list for suggestions:
    Some Current Periodical Indexes
  Business
      Business Periodicals Index, 1958–date
  Fine Arts
      Art Index, 1929–date
      Guide to Dance Periodicals, 1931–date
      Guide to the Performing Arts, 1957–date
      Music Index, 1949–date
  Health and Medicine
      Cumulative Index to Nursing Literature, 1961–date
      Hospital Literature Index, 1955–date
      Index Medicus (National Library of Medicine), 1960–date
      Nursing Studies Index, 1963–date
  Humanities
      British Humanities Index, 1962–date
      Index to Little Magazines, 1948–date
  Law
      Index to Legal Periodicals, 1908–date
  Library Science
      Library Literature, 1921–date
  Religion
      Catholic Periodical Index, 1939–date
      Index to Jewish Periodicals, 1963–date
      Index to Religious Literature, 1949–date

Science and Technology
> *Applied Science and Technology Index* (formerly *Industrial Arts Index*), 1913–date
> *Biological and Agricultural Index* (formerly *Agricultural Index*), 1919–date

Social Sciences
> *America: History and Life*, 1964–date
> *Index to Labor Union Periodicals*, 1960–date
> *Public Affairs Information Service Bulletin*, 1915–date

II. Identify a foreign periodical index which might be useful to you.
III. Malclès' *Bibliography* (New York: Scarecrow Press, Inc., 1961, pp. 85ff.) lists over 100 great retrospective subject bibliographies of the nineteenth century. Identify one of these and explain how it might be useful to you.
IV. Identify one or more of the following:
    A. An index to a newspaper
    B. An index to book reviews
    C. An index to the explication of individual poems
    D. An index (other than a book review index) to criticisms of short stories
    E. An index (other than a book review index) to criticisms of novels
V. Identify one or more of the following:
    A. An index locating individual poems published in collections
    B. An index locating individual speeches published in collections
    C. An index locating individual songs published in collections
    D. An index locating individual short stories published in collections
    E. An index locating individual plays published in collections
VI. Investigate and explain a type of index other than those described in the preceding chapter.
VII. Investigate and report on a new development in the use of the computer in literature searching.

References for the preceding problems

Library Literature, 1921–date. New York: The H.W. Wilson Co., 1934–date.

Malclès, Louise-Noëlle, *Les Sources du Travail Bibliographique*. Genève: E. Droz; Lille: Giard, 1950–58, 4 vols.

Winchell, Constance M., *Guide to Reference Books*. 8th ed. Chicago: American Library Association, 1967; *First Supplement, 1965–1966*. Chicago: American Library Association, 1968.

VII

SCHOLARLY BIBLIOGRAPHY

For out of olde feldes, as men seyth,
Cometh al this newe corn fro yer to yere;
And out of olde bokes, in good feyth,
Cometh al this newe science that men lere.

—*Geoffrey Chaucer*[1]

One of the fastest-growing and most critical areas of subject bibliography is that which deals with the records of scholarship: the books, papers, and journals by means of which scholars on the frontiers of knowledge communicate with one another. The scholarly journal in particular has become a medium for the communication of ideas and methods, and for reporting results of investigations. Since the pages of the *Philosophical Transactions* of the Royal Society of London, in the mid-seventeenth century, first carried communications from learned men of that time, the number of such journals has skyrocketed. A conservative estimate places the number of scientific and technical journals alone at close to 35,000. In the production of knowledge, an enterprise which George Sarton called an "immense collaboration which extends throughout space and time,"[2] it becomes the task of bibliography to arrange these records in such a way that they are readily available, throughout the cycle which begins with a scholar's search of the literature in preparation for an original investigation and ends with the incorporation of his report into the existing literature. For this purpose there exists a complex network of lists, each serving the interests of a par-

---

[1]*The Parliament of Fowls*, lines 22–25
[2]George Sarton, *Introduction to the History of Science* (Baltimore: Published for the Carnegie Institution of Washington by the Williams & Wilkins Company, 1927), Vol. I, p. 31.

ticular group, with little or no coordination among them. Like knowledge itself, this pattern of lists is constantly changing and growing.

Scholarly bibliography seems less chaotic, however, when it is viewed as a part of the total process for the production and dissemination of knowledge. The basic working unit in this process is the discipline. Despite a certain blurring of the boundaries, most scholars affiliate with one or another of the traditional disciplines, read its journals, and attend the meetings of its societies. Because modern bibliographic problems are usually too vast to be soluble, as once they were, by isolated individuals, it is often these societies which have come to the bibliographic rescue, along with universities, governments, and commercial enterprises. The Modern Language Association of America and the American Chemical Society, to name only two, have initiated a wide range of bibliographic activities in their own fields. Occasionally very active subgroups, as, for instance, solid state physicists or Shakespearean scholars, may develop their own specialized bibliographic apparatus within the parent discipline. Although they may differ in their methods and in the materials with which they deal, all disciplines and their subdivisions share a common bibliographic purpose: to make accessible the relevant work of the past to scholars of the present and of the future. This common purpose has generated certain common bibliographic forms which recur in widely different fields.

FORMS OF SCHOLARLY BIBLIOGRAPHY:
ENGLISH LITERATURE

The Retrospective Bibliography

The field of English literature, defined narrowly as the literature of the British Isles, may serve as a first example. For access to the best work of the past in this field the scholar may consult the *Cambridge Bibliography of English Literature*,[3] an outstanding example of a *retrospective bibliography*. It covers the field of British literature from Anglo-Saxon times to the year 1900. As illustrated in Figure 40 it notes bibliographies of an individual author, if such are available, lists his works with their dates, and offers a selection of critical and biographical works about him. The *Cambridge Bibliography* is the work of many scholars, each of whom prepared the bibliography in his own special field. It consists of three volumes and an additional index volume. A supplement issued in 1957 covers

---

[3]*Cambridge Bibliography of English Literature* (New York: Cambridge University Press, 1940–57), 5 vols.

Songs of a Bayadere and Songs of a Trouba-
dour. Dundee, 1893 (priv. ptd).
Selections. Ed. (with introduction) H. S.
Salt, 1925. [With a bibliography.]

(b) Biography and Criticism

Lowe, D. John Barlas: Sweet Singer and
Socialist. Cupar, 1915. [With a bibliography.]

GEORGE BARLOW (1847–1913)

(a) Collected and Selected Works

The Poetical Works of George Barlow. 11
vols. 1902–14.
Selected Poems. 1921. [With introductory
note, signed C. W., a bibliography and a
short life.]

(b) Poems

A Life's Love. 1873. [Sonnets.]
An English Madonna. By James Hinton.
1874.
Under the Dawn. 1875.
The Gospel of Humanity; or, the Connection
between Spiritualism and Modern Thought.
1876.
The Marriage before Death, and Other Poems.
1878.
Through Death to Life. 1878.
Love-Songs. 1880.
Time's Whisperings. Sonnets and Songs.
1880.
Song-Bloom. 1881. [At the end are ptd
extracts from contemporary reviews.]
Song-Spray. 1882.
An Actor's Reminiscences, and Other Poems.
1883.
Love's Offering. By James Hinton. 1883.
Poems Real and Ideal. 1884.
Loved beyond Words. 1885.
The Pageant of Life. An Epic Poem in Five
Books. 1888.
From Dawn to Sunset. 1890.
A Lost Mother. 1892.
The Crucifixion of Man. A Narrative Poem.
1893.
To the Women of England and Other Poems.
1901.
A Coronation Poem. 1902.
Vox Clamantis. Sonnets and Poems. 1904.
A Man's Vengeance and Other Poems. 1908.
Songs of England Awaking. 1909.

(c) Plays

The Two Marriages: a Drama in Three Acts.
1878.
Jesus of Nazareth. 1896. [A tragedy in prose
and verse.]

[Barlow also pbd a novel and various
miscellaneous essays.]

(d) Biography and Criticism

Miles, A. H. George Barlow. Miles, VIII (VII).
Bennett, E. T. The Poetical Work of George
Barlow: a Study. 1903.

JANE BARLOW (1857–1917)

[See p. 1056 below.]

AUBREY VINCENT BEARDSLEY (1872–1898)

(a) Bibliography

Gallatin, A. E. Aubrey Beardsley's Drawings.
1903. [Gives list of books and articles on,
and references to, Beardsley, both as artist
and writer.]

(b) Miscellaneous Writings

Under the Hill and Other Essays in Prose and
Verse. 1904. [Rptd from The Yellow Book
and The Savoy. Under the Hill, The Three
Musicians (a poem), The Ballad of a
Barber (a poem), Carmen CI (a poem),
Table Talk of Beardsley, 2 letters.]
Last Letters. With an Introductory Note by
John Gray. 1904.
The Story of Venus and Tannhäuser. A
Romantic Novel. 1907 (priv. ptd). [The
original, unexpurgated version of Under
the Hill.]

(c) Biography and Criticism

Symons, A. Aubrey Beardsley. 1897; 1905
(rev. and enlarged).
Gallatin, A. E. Whistler's Art Dicta and
Other Essays. 1904. [2 essays on Beards-
ley.]
Ross, R. Aubrey Beardsley. 1909. [A life.]
King, A. W. An Aubrey Beardsley Lecture.
With Introduction by R. A. Walker. 1924.
[Includes 10 letters.]
Macfall, H. Aubrey Beardsley. The Man and
his Work. 1928.

HENRY CHARLES BEECHING (1859–1919)

(a) Bibliography

Stephen, G. A. Bibliography of H. C.
Beeching. Norwich Public Library Readers'
Guide, VII, 1919.

(b) Poems

Mensae Secundae. Oxford, 1879. [By
Beeching, J. W. Mackail and J. B. B.
Nichols.]
Love in Idleness. 1883; 1891 (with addns and
omissions, as Love's Looking Glass. Anon.)
[By Beeching, J. W. Mackail and J. B. B.
Nichols.]
In a Garden, and Other Poems. 1895.
St Augustine at Ostia: Oxford Sacred Poem.
1896.

---

criticism and other secondary materials published up to approximately 1955, although the terminal date for the literature itself remains at 1900.

The Current Bibliography

For records of the scholarship of the more recent past the scholar in English literature may consult a *current bibliography*, such as the *Annual Bibliography of English Language and Literature*.[4] Somewhat broader in scope than the *Cambridge Bibliography*, it includes not only American as well as British literature but also works concerned with the English language. The page shown in Figure 41 comes from the volume for 1955–1956 and includes references to books (6664, 6676), dissertations (6665, 6667), a review (6664), and numerous journal articles, all published during the specified period.

The Review of Research

If the scholar is fortunate he may find a *review of research* for his subject. This will furnish a summary, by an expert in that field, of previous research, often with critical evaluations and insights. It may be an annual review, such as *Year's Work in English Studies*, offering a summary of the scholarship of the preceding year.[5] (Figure 42 shows part of this review devoted to English literature of the twentieth century.) Or the review of research may be more specialized and cover a longer chronological period, as is the case with Houtchens and Houtchens' review of the research concerning certain writers of the romantic period.[6] (Figure 43 shows part of the chapter of this work which reviews Leigh Hunt scholarship.) To make use of such a review is, in effect, to draw upon the knowledge and judgment of a recognized expert in a given field.

The Guide to the Literature

If he is unfamiliar with the bibliography of a subject field the scholar may make use of a *guide to the literature* of that field. This kind of guide is not

---

[4]Modern Humanities Research Association, *Annual Bibliography of English Language and Literature*, 1920–date (Cambridge: Modern Humanities Research Association, 1921–date).

[5]English Association, *Year's Work in English Studies*, 1919/20–date (London: Published for The English Association by John Murray Publishers, Ltd., 1921–date).

[6]Carolyn W. Houtchens and Lawrence H. Houtchens, eds., *The English Romantic Poets and Essayists: A Review of Research and Criticism*, rev. ed. (New York: Published for the Modern Language Association by New York University Press, 1966).

Austen, Jane. 6661. Spence, D. S. White Soup. NQ., Nov. 1955, II (N.S.), 488.

—— **6662.** Trilling, Lionel. The Opposing Self: Nine Essays in Criticism. *See* **2928.**

—— **6663.** Wright, Andrew. A Reply to Mr Burchell on Jane Austen. NCF., Mar. 1956, X, 315–19.

Austin, Alfred. 6664. Crowell, Norton B. Alfred Austin, Victorian. London: Weidenfeld and Nicolson, 1955. pp. 306. 18s. (Cf. Bibl. 1953, 5485.) Rev. by W. L. Burn in 20th Cent., CLIX, 33–43; in Listener, LIV, 431–3.

Bagehot, Walter. 6665. Gronningsater, Arne Howell. Walter Bagehot: A Study of Gradualism as the Condition of Freedom. Unpub. Doct. Diss., Columbia Univ., 1955. [Abstr. in DA., 1955, XV, 2190.]

—— **6666.** Pearson, J. G. The Acute Realism of Walter Bagehot. Listener, Mar. 10, 1955, LIII, 419–20.

Bailey, John. 6666a. Edwards, Oliver. Quiet But True. (John Bailey.) The Times, May 19, 1955, p. 13.

Baillie, Joanna. 6667. Lambertson, Chester Lee. The Letters of Joanna Baillie (1801–1832). Unpub. Doct. Diss., Harvard Univ., 1956.

Barnes, William. 6668. Jacobs, Willis D. William Barnes Linguist. (Univ. of New Mexico Publications in Language and Literature, No. 9.) (Bibl. 1952, 7759.) Rev. by F. Mossé in EA., VIII, 164–5.

6669–70. Entries cancelled.

Baum, L. Frank. 6671. Dempsey, David. The Wizard of Baum. NYTB., May 13, 1956, p. 30.

Beardsley, Aubrey. 6672. Walker, R. A. (ed.). Letters of Aubrey Beardsley. PULC., Spring 1955, XVI, 111–44.

Bellamy, Edward. 6673. Selected Writings on Religion and Society. Edited with an Introduction by Joseph Schiffman. The American Heritage Series, No. 11. N.Y.: Liberal Arts Press, 1955. pp. xlix, 139. $0.75.

Benton, Thomas Hart. 6674. McCandless, Perry. The Political Philosophy and Political Personality of Thomas Hart Benton. Missouri Historical Review, Jan. 1956, L, 145–58.

Besant, Walter. 6675. Boege, Fred W. Sir Walter Besant: Novelist. NCF., Mar. 1956, X, 249–80; *ib.*, June 1956, XI, 32–60.

Bierce, Ambrose. 6676. Fatout, Paul. Ambrose Bierce and the Black Hills. Norman, Oklahoma: Univ. of Oklahoma Press, 1956. pp. xi, 180. $3.50.

—— **6677.** Grenander, M. E. 'Au coeur de la vie'. A French Translation of Ambrose Bierce. BUSE., Winter 1955, I, 237–41.

—— **6678.** Taniguchi, Rikuo. A Study of Ambrose Bierce. Tokyo: Kenkyusha, 1955. pp. 202.

Blackmore, Richard D. 6679. Buckler, William E. Blackmore's Novels before 'Lorna Doone'. NCF., Dec. 1955, X, 169–87.

6680. Entry cancelled.

—— **6681.** Dunn, Waldo Hilary. R. D. Blackmore: A Biography. N.Y.: Longmans, Green; London: Hale, 1956. pp. 316. $5.50; 21s.

The Twentieth Century

MARGARET WILLY and HOWARD SERGEANT

In this chapter books are noticed by Margaret Willy, articles by
Howard Sergeant

BOOKS

1. THE NOVEL

It is chiefly to satisfy their instinctive curiosity, affirms Paul West in the preface to his study of the modern novel,[1] that readers turn to fiction rather than to poetry or philosophy. This curiosity is of three main kinds, which might be defined as social, psychological, and cosmic; and Mr. West's primary concern is with 'the novelist's effort to bring psychology back into proportion with manners, and to augment these two with a view of man in the abstract'. After discussing general principles of fiction, he admirably succeeds in communicating 'something of the adventure of comparing one national tradition with another' in his consideration of the permutations of the form in England (starting with George Moore), France, the United States, Germany, Italy, Spain, and Russia. The chief danger of this type of survey, which encompasses so vast a range of material within a comparatively small space, is degeneration into a superficial catalogue of titles and authors which fails to explore any of its ideas in much depth. West triumphantly avoids this in his lively and lucid study, handling an immense subject with ease, authority, and considerable critical penetration.

The modern novel is also considered by Anthony Burgess in his

concise, astringent essay[2] issued as a supplement to *British Book News*. He writes only of novelists who have published work during the early 60's—both established authors such as Waugh, Snow, Compton-Burnett, and the younger 'angry' group of the 50's, and new-comers like the emerging West Indian and Nigerian novelists. He notes, however, that the period has been 'remarkable less for the emergence of new talent than for the re-emergence of old' (Huxley, Isherwood, Priestley, and Richard Hughes). As always in this series, there is an excellent bibliography.

C. B. Cox in *The Free Spirit*[3] quotes L. P. Hartley's views, in his essay *The Novelist's Responsibility*, on the devaluation of the individual in fiction, as in life, since the last war. The introductory chapter to this study of liberal humanism in a small group of selected novelists poses the problem of the modern liberal's dilemma: the conflict between admiration of active idealism, on the one hand, and on the other an unwillingness to become involved in commitment to any cause which may impinge on his belief in individual liberty. Cox then proceeds to examine

[1] *The Modern Novel*, by Paul West. Hutchinson. pp. xiii + 450. 50s.

[2] *The Novel Today*, by Anthony Burgess. Longmans. (For the British Council and the National Book League.) pp. 56. 2s. 6d.

[3] *The Free Spirit: A Study of Liberal Humanism in the Novels of George Eliot, Henry James, E. M. Forster, Virginia Woolf and Angus Wilson*, by C. B. Cox. O.U.P. pp. 195. 25s.

FIGURE 42. YEAR'S WORK IN ENGLISH STUDIES [*The Year's Work in English Studies*, vol. XLIV (1963), pp. 302–3, published for The English Association by John Murray Publishers, Ltd. Used by permission of the English Association.]

but other works by Boccaccio (*Boccaccio in England from Chaucer to Tennyson,* 1957).

4. ESSAYS

No monograph has been devoted exclusively to Hunt's essays, but they are studied in detail in Landré's second volume. Hunt's reputation as an essayist has declined since the decade following his death. Although certain of his contemporaries indulged in eulogy, the nineteenth-century critics inclined to judge his essays with more discrimination and with the recognition that with all his fine qualities he was probably not one of the very best. Hazlitt, writing "On the Prose-Style of Poets," attributed to Hunt's familiar and miscellaneous papers "all the ease, grace, and point of the best style of Essay-writing"—but with modifications: "Perhaps there is too much the appearance of relaxation and trifling . . . a caprice, a levity, and a disposition to innovate in words and ideas. Still the genuine master-spirit of the prose-writer is there." Although the *Examiner* predicted (3 Sept. 1859) that as an essayist Hunt would never be forgotten, Samuel C. Chew defined his position less glowingly: "Most of his essays and miscellaneous prose writings have proved ephemeral; they were good journalism in their day but are of little moment in ours. He could handle acceptably, and occasionally adorn, any subject that occurred to his quick and facile fancy" (*A Literary History of England,* ed. A. C. Baugh, Vol. IV, 1948).

One of the most substantial periodical articles on Hunt, almost certainly by Gerald Massey (*North British Rev.,* 1860), begins with a long defense intended to offset, for a new generation of readers, the prejudicial effect of earlier unjust criticism. The latter part is mostly extended admiration of Hunt as a prose writer. The essays in the *Indicator, Companion,* and *Seer* are said to "contain the best and fullest expression of his genius" and "place their author in the first rank of English Essayists; the equal companion of Addison and Steele." Edmund Ollier, in his primarily biographical introduction to *A Tale for a Chimney Corner, and Other Essays* (1869), is more restrained and discriminating in his judgments, but regards his selections from the *Indicator* as "among the most admirable essays in the English language."

Arthur Symons has one of the best criticisms in an edition of Hunt's essays and more clearly foreshadows later opinion (introd., *Essays by Leigh Hunt,* 1887). Although he believes that Hunt "has left us little, perhaps nothing, of a secured immortality," the appraisal that follows is discerning, impartial, and appreciative.

FIGURE 43.   THE ENGLISH ROMANTIC POETS AND ESSAYISTS: A REVIEW OF RESEARCH AND CRITICISM [Carolyn W. Houtchens and Lawrence H. Houtchens, *The English Romantic Poets and Essayists* (Rev. ed.; New York: Modern Language Assn., 1966). Used by permission of the publisher.]

to be confused with those bibliographies of special subjects which some-times call themselves guides. The true guide offers a systematic view- of the literature, and for that reason is often prepared for the use of graduate students in a particular subject area. A good example is Bateson's *A Guide to English Literature*[7] (Figure 44). Mr. Bateson, who is also editor of the *Cambridge Bibliography of English Literature*, first points out and describes the important bibliographies, literary histories, and anthologies in the general field of English literature. For each period, from the medieval to the modern, he offers an introductory essay, followed by a list of the outstanding works dealing with that period. His final chapters deal with methods of research in English literature. For a novice in this area, the guide is a means of finding direction in the literature of the field.

SCHOLARLY BIBLIOGRAPHY IN CHEMISTRY: A COMPARISON

It is interesting to compare, bibliographically, the field of English literature, which is relatively stable and oriented toward the past, with that of chemistry, which is advancing so rapidly that it faces an explosion in the volume of its current literature. In the latter field the *retrospective bibliography* assumes less importance. Bolton's *Select Bibliography of Chemistry*, with its supplements, covers works in this field until 1902, but ceases after that date[8] (Figure 45). On the other hand, *current bibliography* in chemistry is highly developed and takes a variety of forms. Instead of the annual bibliography upon which literary scholarship depends, an *abstract journal*, *Chemical Abstracts*, appears at two-week intervals.[9] This journal not only indexes articles but also summarizes them (Figure 46) to help the scholar select those which are relevant. The articles abstracted come from leading chemical journals throughout the world and cover all phases of chemistry. There are indexes by author and by subject as well as by chemical formula and by patent number. As an even more rapid approach to the current literature a new type of index has been developed known as the *current*

---

[7]Frederick W. Bateson, *A Guide to English Literature* (Chicago: Aldine Publishing Company, 1965).

[8]Henry C. Bolton, *Select Bibliography of Chemistry* [1492–1902] Washington: Smithsonian Institution, 1893–1904), 4 vols.

[9]*Chemical Abstracts* (Easton, Pa.: American Chemical Society, 1907–date). *Abstracts of English Studies* (Boulder, Colo.: National Council of Teachers of English, 1958–date) covers the field of English literature, but is not comparable in scope to *Chemical Abstracts*.

IX. A Reading List, 1800–1960

1. BIBLIOGRAPHIES

Volume III of *CBEL* (1940) devotes its 1100 double-column pages entirely to the nineteenth century. With its Supplement (1957) it covers almost every aspect of the period including the Anglo–Irish, Anglo–Indian, English–Canadian, English–South African, Australian, and New Zealand literatures. Unfortunately it is not free from errors. (The second edition will start with this volume.) A more modest affair is the bibliography (of over 200 pages) attached to *The Victorians and After, 1830–1914* by Edith Batho and Bonamy Dobrée (1938). For the major authors the Modern Language Association of America has recently sponsored a "Review of Research" in nineteenth-century English literature, of which 3 volumes have so far appeared—*The English Romantic Poets* (ed. T. S. Raysor, 1950, rev. 1956), *The Victorian Poets* (ed. F. J. Faverty, 1956), and *The English Romantic Poets and Essayists* (ed. C. W. and L. H. Houtchens, 1958). The last item covers Blake, Southey, Campbell, Moore, and Landor, who had been excluded from Volume I (which was restricted to Wordsworth, Coleridge, Byron, Shelley, Keats), as well as Lamb, Hazlitt, Scott, Leigh Hunt, and De Quincey. The Victorian volume covers Tennyson, the Brownings, FitzGerald, Clough, Arnold, Swinburne, the Rossettis, Morris, Hopkins, and fourteen "Later Victorian Poets" (from Meredith to A. E. Housman). *The Victorian Novelists* (ed. Lionel Stevenson) is announced. Each section is by a separate scholar, but the method—a list of recent editions, books, and articles with appropriate comments—is uniform. An anti-critical bias diminishes the value of the series. Lewis Leary's *Contemporary Literary Scholarship* (1958) is less comprehensive, but the chapters on "The Romantic Movement" (by R. H. Fogle) and "The Victorian Period" (by L. Stevenson) are useful for authors outside the scope of the MLA series.

Current work on the period is recorded annually with remarkable thoroughness in two annual bibliographies—"The Romantic Movement" (*ELH*, 1937–49; transferred to *PQ*, 1950–   ), and "Victorian Bibliography" (*MP*, 1933–57; transferred to *Victorian Studies*, 1958–   ). The Victorian bibliographies, 1932–44, were reissued by W. D. Templeman (1945), and those for 1945–54 by A. Wright (1956); both have a general index. Some of the more important works receive brief comments, but these cannot compare with the searching critiques in the 1660–1800 an~~~~~~~~~~~~~~~hies i~~~~~~hich should alwa~~~~

FIGURE 44. BATESON'S A GUIDE TO ENGLISH LITERATURE [Frederick W. Bateson, *A Guide to English Literature* (Chicago: Aldine Publishing Company, 1965). Used by permission of the author.]

SECTION III.

HISTORY OF CHEMISTRY.

INCLUDING THE HISTORY OF ALCHEMY, PHARMACY, PHYSICS, PHO-
TOGRAPHY, TECHNOLOGY, TOXICOLOGY ; DESCRIPTIONS OF LABORA-
TORIES AND REPORTS OF INTERNATIONAL EXPOSITIONS.

AACHEN.
Die chemischen Laboratorien der königlichen rheinisch westfälischen
technischen Hochschule zu Aachen. Mit zwei Blatt Zeichnungen.
Aachen, 1879. 4to.

ABILDGAARD, PETER CHRISTIAN.
Dissertatio critico-chymica de utilitate chymiæ in œconomia reipublicæ.
Hafniæ, 1762.

ACKERMANN, EUGÈNE.
Tableau historique de la découverte des éléments chimiques. Paris,
Juillet, 1888. 1 page folio.
Tableaux scientifiques, No. 6.

AIKIN, ARTHUR.
An Account of the most recent Discoveries in Chemistry and Mineralogy.
London, 1814.

ALMQVIST, C. J. L.
* Anekdoter såsom bidrag till Guldmakariets Historia. Manuskriptet
författadt i St. Louis, Missouri i Norra Amerika, men sedermera
aflemnadt till Törnrosens Bok. Stockholm. *n. d.* pp. 84, 8vo.
The seventh (and last) chapter treats of the adventures of Don Guatimozin,
an alchemist of Missouri and Mexico.

AMBÜHL, G.
Das neue Kantons Laboratorium in St. Gallen. (St. Gallen, Ber. nat.
Ges.) 1886.

AMELUNG, PETER.
Tractatus de alchimiæ sive chemicæ artis inventione et progressione,
obscuratione et instauratione, dignitate, necessitate et utilitate.
Lipsiæ, 1607. 8vo.

85

FIGURE 45. BOLTON'S SELECT BIBLIOGRAPHY OF CHEMISTRY

50548j. Laminating thermoplastic foam to fibrous substrates (Sect. 37) **50721k.** Wax coatings having desirable slip characteristics (Sect. 42) **51056j.** Inorg. oxidizer salt explosive compns. contg. paper sheet particles as pouring-d. reducers (Sect. 50) **51480z.** Basic refractories bonded by hard pitch (Sect. 57) **52890p.**

44—INDUSTRIAL CARBOHYDRATES

S. M. CANTOR

51134h **Molecular structure of starch.** Arturo De Sotgiu. *Corriere Farm.* **22**(7), 165–7(1967)(Ital.). A review of the structure and of the chem. and phys. properties of starch. 7 references.

51135j **Improvements in the method for removal of calcium from molasses.** Saadat A. Khan, Saqib Ahmad, and M. Ikram (North Regional Lab., Pakistan Council Sci. Ind. Res., Peshawar). *Sci. Ind.* (Karachi) **5**(1), 41–4(1967)(Eng). A process is described for reducing the Ca content of cane molasses so that choking of the wash columns during distn. of the molasses does not occur. The molasses are dild. to 40° Brix, adjusted to pH 3.3 with H_2SO_4 or HCl, treated with 5 ml. of 10° Brix Ca superphosphate soln./100 g. of molasses, and heated to 90° for a few sec. The settling time of the ppt. was very short, and clarification by sedimentation gave good results. CNJN

51136k **Effect of heating on the pasting properties of starches.** Gustavo Enrique Perez Mijares (Kansas State Univ., Manhattan). *Diss. Abstr. B* **28**(4), 1297(1967)(Eng). *Univ. Microfilms* (Ann Arbor, Mich.), *Order No.* 66-6485, 69 pp. SNDC

51137m **Studies on plant gums. I. Identification of nitrogenous compounds in neem (Azadirachta indica) gum and isolation of D-glucosamine.** S. Usha Lakshmi and T. N. Pattabiraman (Osmania Univ., Hyderbad, India). *Indian J. Biochem.* **4**(3), 181–3(1967)(Eng). The amino sugar content was detd. in several plant gums, i.e. gum agar, gum shellac, gum myrrha, gum ghatti, gum mastic, carrageenin, neem gum, wood-apple gum, and gum acacia. D-Glucosamine was present only in the neem gum at a concn. of 2.94 ± 0.28 mg./100 g. of the gum. D-Glucosamine was extd. from neem gum and characterized. The

bituric acid (TBA) assay, is independent of the reaction rate, provided the pH is $\geqq 11$. It is concluded that the viscosity decrease and the color in the TBA assay must be caused by the same reaction; a β-alkoxy-elimination reaction. The rate of this reaction for Me alginate is 10^4–10^5 times that of the unesterified alginate. 17 references. RCMW

51141h **The effect of alkali treatment on the chemical heterogeneity and physical properties of some carrageenans.** Olav Smidsroed, Boern Larsen, Alberto J. Pernas, and Arne Haug (Norges Tek. Hogskole, Trondheim, Norway). *Acta Chem. Scand.* **21**(10), 2585–98(1967)(Eng). Alkali treatment markedly influences the wt. distribution of carrageenan fractions with respect to their soly. in KCl solns. All the samples investigated originally contained mols. of widely different solubilities; in most cases, only 2 distinct fractions were present after the treatment, one pptg. below $0.15M$ KCl and one sol. at any KCl concn. up to $1.5M$. Both the chem. and the phys. properties of these 2 fractions varied among the algae. Results are presented to demonstrate that the main effect of the alkali treatment is on the fraction originally pptd. at intermediate KCl concns., leading to a higher content of 3,6-anhydro-D-galactose, a higher gel strength, and a lower soly. The content of 3,6-anhydro-D-galactose cannot, however, be the only factor controlling the soly. level. The results obtained are discussed with view of present knowledge concerning the chem. structure of *Chondrus* carrageenan. The same technique was also applied to furcellaran, phyllophoran, and agar. RCMW

51142j **Nature of unaccounted losses of sugar during diffusion and their determination and prevention.** N. V. Kheize, A. Ya. Zagorul'ko, S. A. Bogdan and T. P. Khval'ko, ..., ...

FIGURE 46. CHEMICAL ABSTRACTS [*Chemical Abstracts*, LXVIII (March 18, 1968), p. 4972. Used by permission of The American Chemical Society.]

awareness index, exemplified by the biweekly publication *Chemical Titles*.[10] It presents a list of titles from some 700 journals, often several months before the abstracts of these same articles appear in *Chemical Abstracts*. Its keyword index allows a scholar to scan all titles containing a particular word (for example, in Figure 47, the word *copper*) and to identify pertinent articles in this way.

In the rapidly expanding field of chemistry the *review of research* is important in summarizing and systematizing the growing volume of work in increasingly specialized fields. Each issue of the quarterly journal, *Chemical Reviews*, carries reviews of research in several areas related to chemistry.[11] An illustration, with part of the accompanying list of references, is shown in Figure 48. Chemistry also has its *guides to the literature*, for example that by Melvin G. Mellon.[12] This guide describes the bibliographic sources for chemistry: primary sources, consisting of periodicals, patent literature, institutional publications; secondary sources, such as bibliographies, works of reference, monographs and textbooks; and tertiary sources, consisting of guides and directories. It also devotes a chapter to methods of making a search of the chemical literature (Figure 49).

The retrospective bibliography, the current bibliography, the review of research, and the guide to the literature occur also in other subject areas, although not all of these forms may be present in every field. Wherever they appear, however, they may serve as guide posts on the trail of scholarly bibliography. As long as a coordinated, centralized system of scholarly bibliography is lacking, such guide posts will be welcome.

---

[10]*Chemical Titles: Current Author and Keyword Indexes from Selected Chemical Journals* (Easton, Pa.: American Chemical Society, 1960–date).

[11]*Chemical Reviews*, 1924–date (Baltimore: Williams and Wilkins, 1925–date).

[12]Melvin G. Mellon, *Chemical Publications, Their Nature and Use*, 4th ed. (New York: McGraw-Hill Book Company, 1965).

```
ACTIVATION CENTERS IN COPPER DOPED POTASSIUM IODIDE          IVUFAC-11-04-151
      BORON PARTICLES IN COPPER DURING NEUTRON IRRADIATION.   JNUMAM-0026-0129
MAGNETIC RESONANCE AND COPPER ELECTRON PARA MAGNETIC         JCPSA6-0048-2689
ESISTIVITY OF BERYLLIUM COPPER FOIL.=    + AND ELECTRICAL R  TMSAAB-0242-0876
           OF ZINC AND COPPER FROM ORGANIC SOLUTIONS AND     ELCAAV-0013-0429
R CORROSION BEHAVIOR OF COPPER IN ACIDS.=    + FEATURES FO   DANTAL-11-02-037
OR THE DETERMINATION OF COPPER IN ALKALINE MEDIUM.=     + F  CHLSAC-0062-0598
         KINETICS OF COPPER IN SILICON NEAR ROOM TEMPER      PHMAA4-0017-0929
GSTATES. PARA MAGNETIC COPPER MOLYBDATE.=       + AND TUN    JCPSA6-0048-2619
DISSOCIATION ENERGY OF COPPER MONO FLUORIDE.=                JCPSA6-0048-2457
OF BERYLLIUM +        COPPER ON THE HARDNESS ANISOTROPY       JNUMAM-0026-0217
FECTS OF TRACE DOSES OF COPPER ON YOUNG AND OLD ANIMALS.=    FATOAO-0031-0226
E OF ALUMINUM OXIDE AND COPPER OXIDES.=       + IN A MIXTUR  OGNPA2-33-04-049
   ON PHOTO CARRIERS IN COPPER PHTHALO CYANINE SINGLE        PHSSAK-0027-0201
PLASTIC DEFORMATION IN COPPER SINGLE CRYSTALS EXPOSED TO     IVUFAC-11-04-047
OF NEUTRON IRRADIATED COPPER SINGLE CRYSTALS.   ACTIVE       PHSSAK-0027-0281
LES+CHRONIC TOXICITY OF COPPER TO FATHEAD MINNOWS (PIMEPHA   WATRAG-0002-0215
RONS IN MUON CAPTURE IN COPPER.=          + YIELD OF NEUT    DANTAL-11-02-019
CT OF GOLD, SILVER, AND COPPER.= + THE PHOTO ELECTRIC EFFE   CHDAAK-266B-1121
N SULFIDE WITH POWDERED COPPER.= + THE REACTION OF HYDROGE   CHDCAQ-0266-1192
TE SOLUTIONS OF IRON IN COPPER-ALUMINUM ALLOYS.= + OF DILU   PYLAAG-0026-0570
   HIGH CONDUCTIVITY OF COPPER-CHROMIUM-LEAD AND COPPER-CH   TMSAAB-0242-0947
                    AND COPPER-CHROMIUM-ZIRCONIUM-LEAD       TMSAAB-0242-0947
TRUCTURE OF THE MASSIVE COPPER-GALLIUM PHASE.=         + S   PHMAA4-0017-0983
COMPENSATION OF IRON IN COPPER-GOLD ALLOYS.=+ VERSUS SPIN    PYLAAG-0026-0502
   OF COPPER-NICKEL AND COPPER-GOLD SYSTEM ALLOYS.=         MTOMAX-68-04-050
STRAIN SENSITIVITY OF COPPER-NICKEL AND COPPER-GOLD         MTOMAX-68-04-050
NUCLE+MODEL SYSTEMS FOR COPPER-PROTEIN INTERACTION.  POLY    ACSAA4-0022-0689
ON BEHAVIOR OF DEFORMED COPPER-SILVER ALLOYS.=+PRECIPITATI   MTLLAF-0022-0405
TERNARY DIFFUSION IN A COPPER-ZINC-TIN SOLID SOLUTIONS.=    TMSAAB-0242-0885
= STACKING FAULTS IN A COPPER-15 AT. PCT. ALUMINUM ALLOY.   PHSSAK-0027-0185
B(PROT                 COPPER-59 AND NICKEL-62(PROTON,PHO    NUPABL-0112-0032
2(PROTON,PHOTON-PHOTON) COPPER-63 REACTIONS.=+AND NICKEL-6   NUPABL-0112-0032
USION OF ATOMS IN GOLD, COPPER, AND ALUMINUM.= + THE DIFF    JOPQAG-0029-0345
OF SUBLIMATED LAYERS OF COPPER, IODIDE, AND CHLORIDE DOPED   ZPSBAX-0008-0638
       PENT OXIDE AND COPPER(I) OXIDE - PHOSPHORUS PENT      JCSIAP-1968-1113
ANODIC DISSOLUTION OF COPPER(I) SULFIDE AND THE DIRECT R     TMSAAB-0242-0780
  OF AMMONIUM COPPER(II)- COPPER(I) SULFIDE.=        CRYSTA  ACSAA4-0022-0581
STRUCTURE OF AMMONIUM COPPER(I) SYSTEMS IN ACETO NITRILE     JEIEBC-0018-0200
ENZENE-M-SULFONATE WITH COPPER(I).=+ DI PHENYL PHOSPHINO B   ACSAA4-0022-0497
MICRO DETERMINATION OF COPPER(II) BROMIDE HYDRATE.=+OF BI    SUKRAJ-0041-0073
NTATE LIGAND FORMED BY+ COPPER(II) BY AN EXCHANGE REACTION   MIACAQ-1968-0664
POLY NUCLEAR COPPER(II) COPPER(II) COMPLEXES OF A QUADRIDE   JCSIAP-1968-1265
NICKEL(II), AND COPPER(II) COMPLEXES OF GLYCYL             ACSAA4-0022-0689
IDINES.=               COPPER(II) COMPLEXES OF 4(5)-BROMO    JCSIAP-1968-1189
NE-N,N,+POLAROGRAPHY OF COPPER(II) COMPLEXES WITH SUBSTITU   IJNOCA-0006-0112
S(1,2-PROPANE DI AMINE) COPPER(II) CYCLO HEXANE-1,2-DI AMI   JEIEBC-0018-0151
BIS(ETHYLENE DI AMINE) COPPER(II) DI CHROMATE(VI).=+OF BI    SUKBAJ-0041-0063
IN AQUEOUS SOLUTIONS OF COPPER(II) FLUORO BORATE.=    + OF   ACRCAR-0024-0730
SPIN RESONANCE STUDY OF COPPER(II) ION AND 2,2'-DI PYRIDIN   JCPSA6-0048-2689
IN THE SYSTEMS COPPER(II) COPPER(II) ION IN SILVER CHLORIDE  PHSSAK-0027-077K
FORMED BY REACTION OF COPPER(II) OXIDE - PHOSPHORUS PENT     JCSIAP-1968-1113
ES AND BASIC HALIDES OF COPPER(II) 2-HYDROXY ETHYL AMINE     JCSIAP-1968-1265
ION OF BIS(TETRAZOLATO) COPPER(II).=    + STUDIES ON HALID   JCSIAP-1968-1417
LO TRI ACETIC ACID WITH COPPER(II).=+ ION AND THE PREPARAT   JACSAT-0090-2518
POTENTIALS OF COPPER(II).=+ THE COMPLEX OF NITRI            JACSAT-0090-2514
ON THE SPECIFIC HEAT OF COPPER(II)-COPPER(I) SYSTEMS IN      JEIEBC-0018-0200
ORDERED AND DISORDERED COPPER(3)-GOLD BELOW 3-DEG.-K.=      CJPHAD-0046-0923
IN COPPER(5)-ZINC(8), COPPER(3)-GOLD.=    + MECHANISMS IN    PHMAA4-0017-0999
      OF ATOMS IN COPPER(5)-ZINC(8), COPPER(5)-CADMI       ACSAA4-0022-0653
PPER(5)-CADMIUM(8), AND COPPER(9)-ALUMINUM(4).=       + CO   ACSAA4-0022-0653
PROTOPORPHYRIN IX FROM COPROPORPHYRINOGEN III BY BACTERIA    BIJOAK-0107-0446
RANSFERASE IN UMBILICAL CORD BLOOD.=       + PHOSPHO T       CCATAR-0020-0465
MOLECULE USING AN ARC CORD IN THE AXIALLY VORTICAL AIR      OPSPAM-0024-0506
ONSTITUENTS OF SYZYGIUM CORDATUM.=                      C    PYTCAS-0007-0889
TE. COMPOUND WITH FIVE CORDINATE MOLYBDENUM(VI).=+MOLYBDA    JCSIAP-1968-1398
AND YTTRIUM OXIDE ON A CORE FROM UR-20 ALLOY.= + DI OXIDE    IUZFAU-12-01-034
         KIHARA CORE MODEL FOR POLAR MOLECULES.=            JPCHAX-0072-1821
N-15 AND NITROGEN-15.= CORE POLARIZATION EFFECTS IN OXYGE    NUPABL-0112-0296
ND THE DETERMINATION OF CORIOLIS COEFFICIENT ZETA(33).=+ A   CJPHAD-0046-0977
SQUARE PYRAMIDAL MOLEC+ CORIOLIS COUPLING COEFFICIENTS OF    CUSCAN-0037-0252
HENIUM TETR OXIDE.  + CORIOLIS COUPLING CONSTANTS OF RUT     JMOSA3-0026-0136
NATION OF TRYPTOPHAN IN CORN (ZEA MAYS).=         DETERMI    JAFCAU-0016-0514
S IN SEVERAL STRAINS OF CORN (ZEA MAYS).=    + INTERACTION   AGJOAT-0060-0267
AMINO AZO BENZENE AND CORN OIL ON AZO DYE REDUCTASE IN       BIJOAK-0107-015PR
OF EXOGENOUS SUCROSE BY CORN SCUTELLUM SLICES.=   STORAGE    PYTCAS-0007-0701
EA (DIURON)) APPLIED TO CORN SEEDLINGS.=      + METHYL UR    JAFCAU-0016-0426
AND L(+)-LACTIC ACID IN CORN SILAGE.=+ TREATMENT ON D(-)-    JDSCAE-0051-0802
OF CROTHILIN UPON CORN UNDER VARIOUS PHOSPHORUS AND         ITSAA7-68-02-087
BOILING (TO A PULP) OF CORN.= + AMYLASE FOR IMPROVING THE    FSPMAM-34-03-015
E OF ITS METABOLITES IN CORN, GRASS, AND MILK.=  + AND FIV   JAFCAU-0016-0399
APHIC LAYERS.=         CORONA CHARGING BEHAVIOR OF XEROGR    PSENAC-0012-0165
E, ON FAT +            CORONARY ACTIVE COMPOUND, VISNADIN    ARZNAD-0018-0309
IPYRIDAMOLE ON REGIONAL CORONARY RESISTANCE.=       + AND D  CIRUAL-0022-0649
HOLE STEROL ESTERASE IN CORPUS LUTEUM.=                 C    BIJOAK-0107-020PR
AN INTERNAL STANDARD TO CORRECT FOR CHOLE STEROL LOSSES IN   JLPRAW-0009-0374
AND PHYSIOLOGICAL CORRELATES OF THE LOSS OF KINETOPL         JCLBA3-0037-0660
PHOSPHATE COMPLEXES AND CORRELATIONS FOR METAL-SULFUR        JCSIAP-1968-1299
NO REACTIO+POLARIZATION CORRELATIONS IN HIGH ENERGY NEUTRI   PHRVAO-0168-1662
NG TREATMENT OF PAIRING CORRELATIONS IN NUCLEI.=+ CONSERVI   NCIBAW-0055-0185
ON,PHOTON-PHOTON+TRIPLE CORRELATIONS IN THE NICKEL-58(PROT   NUPABL-0112-0032
STEROID MASS SPECTRAL CORRELATIONS.  HYDROXY PROGE STERO     JOCEAH-0033-1740
STRUCTURE REACTIVITY CORRELATIONS.  REACTIVITY OF N+        JACSAT-0090-2623
```

FIGURE 47. CHEMICAL TITLES [*Chemical Titles*, June 3, 1968, p. 26. Used by permission of The American Chemical Society.]

FULVENES AND SUBSTITUTED FULVENES

(4) Agranat, I., and Bergmann, E. D., *Tetrahedron Letters*, 2373 (1963).
(5) Alder, K., Braden, R., and Flock, F. H., *Ber.*, **94**, 456 (1961).
(6) Alder, K., Chambers, F. W., and Trimborn, W., *Ann.*, **566**, 27 (1950).
(7) Alder, K., Flock, F. H., and Beumling, H., *Ber.*, **93**, 1896 (1960).
(8) Alder, K., and Ruehmann, R., *Ann.*, **566**, 1 (1950).
(9) Alder, K., and Stein, G., *Angew. Chem.*, **50**, (1937).
(10) Allinger, N. L., *Tetrahedron*, **22**, 1367 (1966).
(11) Altman, J., and Wilkinson, G., *J. Chem. Soc.*, 5654 (1964).
(12) Andreades, S., *J. Chem. Soc.*, **87**, 3941 (1965).
(13) Angus, H. J. F., McDonald Blair, J., and Bryce-Smith, D., *J. Chem. Soc.*, 2003 (1960).
(14) Angus, H. J. F., and Bryce-Smith, D., *J. Chem. Soc.*, 1409 (1960).
(15) Arcus, C. L., and Coombs, M. M., *J. Chem. Soc.*, 4319 (1954).
(16) Atkinson, E. R., Levins, P. L., and Dickelman, T. E., *Chem. Ind.* (London), 934 (1964).
(17) Avramoff, M., and Sprinzak, Y., *J. Am. Chem. Soc.*, **82**, 4958

FULVENES AND SUBSTITUTED FULVENES

ERNST D. BERGMANN

Institute for Advanced Study, Princeton, New Jersey

Received April 12, 1967

CONTENTS

FIGURE 48. CHEMICAL REVIEWS [Reprinted from *Chemical Reviews*, vol. 68, February 1968, pp. 41, 77. Copyright 1968 by the American Chemical Society. Reprinted by permission of the copyright owner.]

British Abstracts. The two journals just described are the main current ones devoted entirely to general abstracts, but many others contain abstracts along with other material. Two of these deserve special attention because of their general nature. They are the *Journal of the Chemical Society* (London) and the *Journal of the Society of Chemical Industry* (London). Abstracts appeared first in the former journal in 1871, and a separate volume was devoted to them first in 1878. From then until 1926 the even-numbered volume for each year was devoted to abstracts on general, organic, and physical chemistry. The latter journal was started in 1882 and from the beginning included abstracts on all aspects of applied chemistry.

Beginning in 1926 the abstracting work of the two journals was combined in *British Chemical Abstracts, Part A,* pure chemistry, bound separately, and Part *B,* applied chemistry, bound as part of the *Journal of the Society of Chemical Industry* (name changed to *Chemistry and Industry*). Later the abstracting name was changed to *British Chemical and Physiological Abstracts,* and finally, in 1945, to *British Abstracts.* In 1944 Part *C,* Analysis and Equipment, was added. All the parts had subparts, generally paged separately. Finally, in 1953, this fine abstracting service was terminated.

The general quality of these English abstracts was high. Together they enable one to follow abstracts in the English language back to the dates given. *Chemical Abstracts* consistently covered more periodicals. The indexes available are shown in the accompanying table. A list of periodicals abstracted was published in 1949.

Since 1953 what is left of *British Abstracts* appears in the following two journals:

1. *Journal of Applied Chemistry.* The abstracts are classified under (1) Chemical Engineering and Atomic Energy; (2) Fuel and Fuel Products; (3) Industrial Inorganic Chemistry; (4) Industrial Organic Chemistry; (5) Fats, Waxes, Detergents; (6) Fibres; and (7) Laboratory Apparatus and Technique; Unclassified.

2. *Analytical Abstracts.* The abstracts are classified under (1) General Analytical Chemistry, (2) Inorganic Analysis, (3) Organic Analysis, (4) Biochemistry (five subdivisions), (5) General Technique and Laboratory Apparatus (five subdivisions).

Bulletin de la société chimique de France. This journal first included abstracts in 1863. From 1892 to 1933 even-numbered volumes contained the abstracts. Since that time this volume has been known as the "documentation volume." Since 1918 French abstracts on applied chemistry have appeared in *Chimie & industrie* (Paris).

FIGURE 49. MELLON'S CHEMICAL PUBLICATIONS: THEIR NATURE AND USE [Melvin G. Mellon, *Chemical Publication, Their Nature and Use* (4th ed.; New York: McGraw-Hill Book Company, Inc., 1965). Used by permission of the publisher.]

SUGGESTIONS FOR FURTHER INVESTIGATION

I. Can you identify an example of a retrospective bibliography in your field of interest? A current bibliography? A review of research? A guide to the literature?

II. Can you discover forms of scholarly bibliography, other than the four mentioned in *I*, which are common to two or more disciplines or subject fields? Identify examples.

III. Construct a *guide to the literature* of a well-defined subject area in which you are interested and for which no such guide exists. The two guides mentioned in this chapter, Bateson (7) and Mellon (12), may be used as examples.

References for the preceding problems

Malclès, Louise-Noëlle, *Les Sources du Travail Bibliographique*. Genève: E. Droz; Lille: Giard, 1950–58, 4 vols.

White, Carl M., ed., *Sources of Information in the Social Sciences*. Totowa, N.J.: Bedminister Press, 1964.

Winchell, Constance M., *Guide to Reference Books*. 8th ed. Chicago: American Library Association, 1967; *First Supplement, 1965–1966*. Chicago: American Library Association, 1968.

VIII

BIBLIOGRAPHIC CITATION

A man will turn over half a library to make one book.

—Samuel Johnson[1]

No study of the orderly presentation of records would be complete which failed to consider the process by which the scholar presents the sources of his work. One of the hallmarks of scholarly writing, in fact, is its use of documentation in the form of the bibliographies and footnotes which acknowledge its sources. Modern scholarship demands scrupulous honesty in attributing credit for borrowed words and thoughts, for these are a scholar's property and his means of livelihood. Even if there were no copyright laws to protect them, honesty and courtesy would demand their acknowledgement.

THE LIST OF REFERENCES

The chief reason for the documentation of scholarly work, however, lies in the fact that such work must be open to challenge and testing. Whoever would challenge it needs access to the sources used. It is customary, therefore, for a bibliography or list of references to form part of a piece of scholarly work. In the bibliography which accompanies his study of the Spanish Civil War (Figure 50), Hugh Thomas takes the reader back through the documents, memoirs, and even novels which he examined in

---

[1] *Boswell's Life of Dr. Johnson* (Everyman edition), vol. 1, p. 545.

constructing his own version of the event.² The list is divided into the following sections:

Documents
Leading Memoirs
Other Memoirs
Leading Contemporary Pamphlets and Polemics, *etc.*
Contemporary Accounts
Later Accounts
General Works
Novels
Encyclopedias
Newspapers and Periodicals

Arrangement

Because the bibliography runs to approximately twenty-five pages, this division is necessary to show at a glance the kinds of sources used. The author might have arranged his references in a single list by authors' names if this had suited his purpose. He might have arranged the list by dates of publication if he had wished to show the rise and decline of interest in the subject, or by the nationality of the authors if he had wanted to demonstrate the involvement of citizens of foreign countries in this war. He might have divided his bibliography into sections on The Political Background, The International Brigades, The Role of the Church, and so forth, to emphasize these aspects. If he had wanted to comment on his sources he might have written a bibliographic essay like the following:

A brilliant but superficial account of Nechayev and his followers is given in V.P. Kozmin, *Nechayev i Nechayevtsi*, Moscow, 1931. . . . For an account of Nechayev's childhood I am indebted to N.C. Belchikov's brief monograph, *S.G. Nechayev v sele Ivanove v 60–e gody*, which appeared in *Katorga i Ssylka* in 1925. There exists an excellent study of the *Revolutionary Catechism* in A.A. Shilov, *Katechesis revolutsionera k istorii nechayevskogo dela*, which appeared in *Borba Klassov* in 1924. I have based the present translation of the *Revolutionary Catechism* on the authoritative version printed by order of the Czarist government in *Pravitelstvenniye Vyestnik*, for July 11, 1871. Other issues of the newspaper give verbatim accounts of the trial of Nechayev's followers, from which it is possible to reconstruct the murder of Ivanov. I have delved into the memoirs of Herzen and Ralli-Arbore for details of Nechayev's visits to Switzerland, and I owe a particular debt to M.P. Sazhin's

²Hugh Thomas, *The Spanish Civil War* (New York: Harper & Row, Publishers, 1961).

CHURCHILL, WINSTON, *The Second World War, Vol. I: The Gathering Storm (London 1948).

CIANO, COUNT GALEAZZO, *Diplomatic Papers (edited Malcolm Muggeridge) (London 1948); *Diary 1937–38 (edited Malcolm Muggeridge) (London 1952); *Diary 1939–43 (edited Malcolm Muggeridge) (London 1947).

COT, PIERRE, *The Triumph of Treason [tr.] (New York 1944).

*Epistolario Negrín y Prieto (Paris 1939).

FEILING, KEITH, *The Life of Neville Chamberlain (London 1946).

GALLAND, GENERAL ADOLF, *The First and the Last [tr.] (Preface by Douglas Bader) (London 1955).

GAMELIN, GENERAL GEORGES, *Servir (3 vols.) (Paris 1946–7).

GAMIR ULÍBARRI, GENERAL, *De Mis Memorias (Paris 1939).

GARCÍA PRADAS, JOSÉ, *Cómo termino la Guerra de España (Buenos Aires 1940). See also Section IV.

GARCÍA-VALIÑO Y MARCÉN, GENERAL RAFAEL, *Guerra de Liberación Española. Campañas de Aragón y Maestrazgo (Madrid 1949).

GONZÁLEZ, VALENTÍN (El Campesino), * Listen Comrades! (London 1952); *Comunista en España y anti-Stalinista en Rusia (Mexico 1953).

GORKIN, JULIÁN (Julián Gómez), *Cannibales Políticos: Hitler y Stalin en España (Mexico 1941).

un Trono (Madrid 1932) (English tr. The fall of a Throne, London 1933).

'ANDRÉS DE PALMA', *Mallorca en la Guerra contra el Marxismo (Palma de Mallorca 1936).

ARMILLAS GARCÍA, LUIS (with MANUEL MONTELLA MUÑOZ), Rutas Gloriosas (Cádiz 1939).

ARMIÑÁN ODRIOZOLA, L. DE, Por los Caminos de Guerra (Madrid 1939).

ARSENIO DE IZARGA Y OJEMBARRENA, G., Los Presos de Madrid (Madrid 1940).

AVILÉS G., Tribunales Rojos vistos por un Abogado Defensor (Barcelona 1939).

BAHAMONDE Y SÁNCHEZ DE CASTRO, ANTONIO, *Memoirs of a Spanish Nationalist (London 1939).

BAJATIERRA, MAURO, Cronicas del Frente de Madrid (Barcelona 1937).

BALBONTÍN, JOSÉ ANTONIO, La España de mi Experiencia (Mexico 1952).

BALK, THEODOR (editor), La Quatorzième (Madrid 1937).

BARAIBAR, CARLOS DE, La Guerra de España en el Plano Internacional (Barcelona 1937).

BARBERÁ SABORIDO, M., Impresiones de un Año (Barcelona 1937).

BAREA, ARTURO, *The Clash (London 1946).

FIGURE 50. PART OF BIBLIOGRAPHY ACCOMPANYING THOMAS' THE SPANISH CIVIL WAR [Hugh Thomas, The Spanish Civil War (New York: Harper and Row, Publishers, 1961). Used by permission of the author.]

memoirs: *Vospominaniya, 1860–1880*, Moscow, 1925. For the rest it is only necessary to add that Nechayev dominated the thoughts of most of the terrorists who lived at the end of the last century, and nearly all of them have recorded minor details of his exploits.[3]

A scholarly bibliography need not be arranged according to a prescribed pattern. Rather, it is flexible, and may be made to serve the purposes of the author. It may and should, however, adapt to the needs of the reader. One of the greatest benefits which the author can confer upon this unknown being, bibliographically speaking, is to smooth his path from the entry in the bibliography or in the footnote to the book on the shelf, and this is accomplished by a description which allows no possiblity for mistaken identity. The problem of bibliographic citation, in fact, is essentially one of identification.

Bibliographic Description

Bibliographic description can, when necessary, be very exact. Figure 51 illustrates the detailed description of a book as it is recorded in the accepted shorthand of professional bibliographers.[4] Here the title page, usually regarded as the source of official information about a book, is reproduced almost as exactly as if in facsimile. Even the typeface corresponds to that of the original page. The slashes after the words *Peace, Tolstoy, etc.*, indicate the end of line of print on this page. The decoration is described. Then follows the collation, or physical description of the book: the size and the number of signatures (sections of pages),[5] and the number of leaves and pages. The notes which follow describe the contents of each preliminary page and the locations of various headings. Description of the text includes the typeface and kind of paper used. The binding and the endpapers are described. With such exact description there would seem to be little chance of mistaking this book for another.

ELEMENTS OF IDENTIFICATION

Detailed bibliographic descriptions can prove extremely useful in the field of rare books, where a comma turned upside down may double the price of

---

[3]Pierre Stephen Robert Payne, *The Terrorists: The Story of The Forerunners of Stalin* (New York: Funk and Wagnalls, 1957), pp. 351–52.

[4]Fredson T. Bowers, *Principles of Bibliographical Description* (Princeton: Princeton University Press, 1949), p. 486.

[5]In this case, 36 signatures of 16 leaves each (a leaf being one sheet, equal to two pages), unsigned, i.e, not marked to indicate their sequence.

binding: maroon pebbled cloth, front and back covers blank. On spine: ivory paper label [in <u>blue</u> and black] **Gibbon** || THE | ROMAN | EMPIRE | I [II *etc.*]

End-paper front and back, coated on front side deep purple. Binder's leaf front and back, its conjugate pasted under lining-paper.

White wove unwatermarked paper; top edges cut and gilt; other edges unopened.

Notes: [these would discuss the editing of the text and the use of notes and material from various earlier sources, the previous appearances of the preliminary critical and biographical material, the date of the printing, and the history of the plates from which the impression was printed]

TOLSTOY, War and Peace [1931]

WAR AND PEACE | A NOVEL BY COUNT LEO TOLSTOY | [decorative rule] | TRANSLATED FROM THE RUSSIAN | BY CONSTANCE GARNETT | [Modern Library device] | [dec. rule] | BENNETT A. CERF · DONALD S. KLOPFER | THE MODERN LIBRARY | NEW YORK

Coll: (8 1/32×5 13/32): [unsigned: 1–36^{16}], 576 leaves, pp. [4] 1–1146 *1147–1148*.

prp. [*1*]: *half-title*, 'THE MODERN LIBRARY | *of the World's Best Books* | [dec. rule] | WAR AND PEACE'. prp. [*2*]: *pub. adv. for The Modern Library (8 lines) between single short dec. rules*. prp. [*3*]: *title*. prp. [*4*]: [short dec. rule] | 'A PUBLISHER'S NOTE | ON THIS EDITION OF | WAR AND PEACE | [13 lines] | [short dec. rule] | *Manufactured in the United States of America | Bound for* THE MODERN LIBRARY *by H. Wolff*. p. 1: *text, headed Part I*. p. 1012: *Part XV*. p. 1062: *EPILOGUE | Part I*. On p. 1146: *THE END*. pp. *1147–1148*: blank.

Text: 10-pt. solid linotype condensed old style. White wove unwatermarked paper, all edges cut, top-edge stained red.

Binding: red cloth, horizontal grain. Front cover: device, naked runner with torch over double rule, stamped in silver. Spine: [stamped in silver] [decorative double rule] | *War | and Peace* | TOLSTOY | [dec. double rule] | MODERN | LIBRARY Back cover: blank. Off-white end-paper front and back.

FIGURE 51. A DETAILED BIBLIOGRAPHICAL DESCRIPTION [Fredson T. Bowers, *Principles of Bibliographical Description* (Princeton, N.J.: Princeton University Press, 1949): part of p. 486. Used by permission of the publisher.]

a book and where forgeries are not unknown. They also have their uses in establishing the authorship or authenticity of a text. Most scholarly work, however, is more concerned with the content of books than with their physical features, and a simpler type of description suffices. In the Thomas bibliography on the Spanish Civil War (Figure 50), four elements of identification are consistently used: the author's name, the title of the book, the place of publication, and the date of publication.

The Author

The first element, *the author*, is usually regarded as the most important element in the description of a book, representing as it does the person responsible for the book's contents. The importance of the names of the authors of the memoirs in Thomas' bibliography is obvious. He treats them with respect, printing them in capital letters and giving full names in most cases rather than initials. The author alone, however, is rarely enough to identify a particular book unless, like Marcel Proust, he is known for only one. Even so, it is likely to be an imprecise sort of identification. Which edition, which translation of *A la Recherche du Temps Perdu* is indicated by citing the name of Proust?

The Title

The second element, *the title*, may also, on occasion, identify a work. *The Bible* and *The Arabian Nights* define particular works, but leave unspecified a world of editions and translations. Often the title helps the reader make a preliminary judgment about a book by revealing its bias as, for example, *The Triumph of Treason*, by Pierre Cot.

The Place of Publication

The addition of the third element, *the place of publication*, continues to refine the description, at the same time providing a further aid to a preliminary judgment. In Thomas' bibliography the number of memoirs published in foreign countries emphasizes the difference which might be expected between a report of this war published in Madrid and one published in exile in Mexico or France.

The Date of Publication

The fourth element, *the date of publication*, also refines the description and helps the reader to make a judgment. In relation to the memoirs of the Spanish Civil War it indicates the book's proximity in time to the event and thus serves as a rough indicator of its reliability and objectivity.

Together these four elements of identification describe a book with enough precision for most purposes. If more bibliographic information is needed, these elements are sufficient to locate the item in a trade bibliography, library catalog, or other source which can supply the missing data. The following item from Thomas' bibliography, for example:

Cot, Pierre. *The Triumph of Treason* (tr.) (New York: 1944)

can readily be located in the *Cumulative Book Index, 1943–1948* where it appears as follows:

Cot, Pierre. Triumph of Treason (tr. by Sybille and Milton Crane) (Alliance bk) 0 432 p. $3.50 Ziff-Davis; $4.50 Ambasador bks.

Additional Elements of Identification

It is often convenient for the reader to be furnished with some of the following additional elements of identification:
The name of the publisher:

Thomas, Hugh, *The Spanish Civil War*. New York: Harper & Row, Publishers, 1961.

The number of pages or volumes:

Adamson, David Grant, *The Kurdish War*. New York: Frederick A. Praeger, Inc., 1965, 215 pp.

Roosevelt, Franklin Delano, *Public Papers and Addresses*. New York: Random House, Inc., 1938–50. 13 vols.

The series of which the book is a part:

Kurtz, Benjamin Putnam, *From St. Antony to St. Guthlac*. University of California Publications in Modern Philology XII, 2. Berkeley: University of California Press, 1926.

The edition:

Chiang, I., *Chinese Calligraphy: An Introduction to Its Aesthetic and Technique.* 2d ed. Cambridge, Mass.: Harvard University Press, 1954.

The editor:

Azaña y Diaz, Manuel, *Memorias Intimas.* Edited by Joaquin Arraras. Madrid: 1939.

The translator:

Casada, Colonel Segismundo, *The Last Days of Madrid.* Tr. Ruper Croft-Cooke. London: 1939.

The illustrator:

Dobie, James Frank, *Apache Gold and Yaqui Silver.* Illustrated by Tom Lea. Boston: Little, Brown and Company, 1939.

Explanatory or critical notes:

Gordon, Sydney, *The Scalpel, The Sword.* (Life of Dr. Norman Bethune) London: 1954.
Judd, Sylvestre, *Margaret, A Tale of the Real, the Ideal, Blight and Bloom; Including Sketches of a Place Not Before Described, Called Mons Christi.* Boston: Jordan and Wiley, 1845.
The first edition was charged with being too frank. The 1851 edition is much less vigorous, somewhat less polished, and not at all earthy or frank.

Essentially the same elements, with varying degrees of emphasis and some few additions, serve to identify sources other than books. For the periodical article, for instance, the place of publication assumes less importance, while the name of the periodical, volume, date, and pages are needed to complete the citation.

Claussen, W. Edmunds, "Bonanza at Old Baldy." *New Mexico,* XXV (May 1947), 14–15.

With a government publication the author may be a division of government rather than a person, but the exact name of this division is important for identification. The series, if any, should be included in identifying a government publication, for this may prove to be an important clue. Date of publication is also important, but the publisher may be assumed if it is the government.

U.S. Public Health Service, *The Health Consequences of Smoking.* Public Health Service Publications No. 1696. Washington: 1967.

For a thesis or dissertation the name of the institution for which it was written becomes an important element of identification.

Lekachman, Robert, "Competition in Commercial Printing." Doctoral dissertation, Columbia University, 1954.

Other unpublished sources such as interviews or letters present special problems which can usually be resolved by considering the elements which a reader needs to identify and locate these sources.

THE FOOTNOTE

On occasion an author may want to cite not only an entire work but a specific page of that work as a source or authority. He may do this by using some such phrase as "as W.L. Jones states in his *All the World's a Stage* (published in New York by Columbia University Press in 1919), on page 17." Too many such asides, however, may distract the reader from the substance of the work. For this reason the author may choose to embody the same information in a footnote. The term footnote applies to any note to which reference is made from the text, whether it is located at the foot of the page or elsewhere. Footnotes are of three kinds: the content note which explains and amplifies the author's thought, the cross reference note which refers the reader to another part of the same work, and the bibliographic note which cites authority or acknowledges sources for particular statements. The bibliographic footnote, like the entry in the bibliography, must also describe a work in sufficient detail to identify it, and it makes use of the same elements of identification. However, the footnote reference assumes a slightly different form. Following is a reference as it might appear in the bibliography:

Roethke, Theodore, *Collected Poems.* Garden City, N.Y.: Doubleday & Company, Inc., 1966.

In a footnote the same work would appear as follows:

Theodore Roethke, *Collected Poems* (Garden City, N.Y.: Doubleday & Company, Inc., 1966), p. 89.

The reasons for these variations lie in the different functions of the bibliography and the footnote. The entry in the bibliography is an item in a list, and the surname of the author very likely determines the position of the entry. Therefore it is placed first, with all following lines indented. The elements of identification within the entry are items in a subsidiary list and are punctuated to show this relationship. The footnote citation, on the other hand, is in effect an abbreviated sentence which says: "Refer to this author, in his book by this title (published in this place: by this publisher, in this year), on this page." Because it does not form part of a list there is no need to invert the author's name or to give it a prominent position by indenting the succeeding lines.

Avoiding Repetition in the Footnote

Some symbol or device within the text, commonly a superior number, is used to refer the reader to the appropriate note. This may be at the foot of the page or, perhaps, at the end of the chapter or book. Constant reference to the same sources may result in a considerable amount of repetition of the elements of identification for these sources. One method of avoiding such repetition consists of describing the work fully in the first citation and thereafter referring to this citation by means of one of the following Latin expressions:[6]

>   *ibidem* (abbreviated *ibid.*), meaning "in the same place"
>   *opere citato* (abbreviated *op. cit.*), meaning "in the work cited"
>   *loco citato* (abbreviated *loc. cit.*), meaning "in the place cited"

Figures 52,[7] 53,[8] and 54[9] show the use of these abbreviations in footnotes.

   Another means of avoiding repetition is the use of terminal notes. The list of references is placed at the end of the work, arranged in a convenient order, and numbered, with each item fully described. Reference is then made from the text to the list, as necessary. Figure 55 illustrates the use of terminal notes.

---

[6]When references to the same work do not closely follow each other, however, it is more convenient to repeat the author's name. For example: Richardson, VII, 301.

[7]Richard P. Stevens, *American Zionism and U.S. Foreign Policy* (New York: Pageant Press, 1962), p. 37.

[8]Manfred Jonas, *Isolationism in America, 1935–1941* (Ithaca, N.Y.: Cornell University Press, 1966), p. 14.

[9]Robert A. Dahl, *Congress and Foreign Policy* (New York: Harcourt, Brace & World, Inc., 1950), p. 226.

III   THE POLITICAL FRONT—1944

Palestine resolution proposed.—The existence of a revitalized Emergency Council quickly produced political repercussions in Washington. The most important step on the political front was the introduction of the Palestine resolutions in both Houses of Congress. "The technical or strategic purpose of this move was to set up a specific target upon which the Council could effectively concentrate the fire of its propaganda." [1] The Council realized that such a move involved risks, but it "had become convinced that the risk of inaction was even greater." [2] Since members of Congress tend to be responsive to pressure groups, it was not surprising that such a program was launched. Besides, a long history of political declarations expressing sympathy towards Jewish development of Palestine had brought little organized opposition. It could therefore be assumed by most legislators that a pro-Palestine stand would only strengthen their positions. Two identical measures concerning Palestine were therefore introduced on January 27, 1944, in the House of Representatives and read as follows:

---

1. ZOA, *47th Annual Report*, p. 61.
2. *Ibid.*

37

FIGURE 52. USE OF *ibid*. THE SECOND FOOTNOTE REFERS TO THE SAME WORK AS THE NOTE IMMEDIATELY PRECEDING. [Richard P. Stevens, *American Zionism and U.S. Foreign Policy* (New York: Pageant Press, 1962), p. 37. Used by permission of the author.]

The geographic position of the United States and the distribution of power among the nations of the world during the nineteenth century made it possible for this country to pursue what it considered its best interests without directly aligning itself with any nation or bloc. In a limited sense, such a course may be regarded as one of isolation. But it can be more accurately defined as the achievement, to an enviable degree, of the ability to act independently in foreign affairs.

"It is," as President Grover Cleveland explained in 1885, "the policy of independence, favored by our position and defended by our known love of justice and by our power. It is the policy of peace suitable to our interests. It is the policy of neutrality, rejecting any share in foreign broils and ambitions upon other continents and rejecting their intrusion here. It is the policy of Monroe and of Washington and of Jefferson—'Peace, commerce and honest friendship with all nations; entangling alliances with none.' "[18]

The isolationists of the 1930's believed that the conditions of their time were still suitable for such a policy. They realized that some things had changed. The United States had developed into a major power and acquired overseas possessions. Rapid means of transportation and communication posed problems that had not existed in the nineteenth century, and military technology had made frightening progress. But they were convinced that the possible effects of these changed conditions could be neutralized by adopting precautionary domestic legislation and cultivating proper attitudes in the American people.

In the course of adapting their concept of foreign policy to the requirements of the twentieth century, they were compelled to espouse schemes tending to abridge the commercial ties which Washington and Jefferson had deemed essential

[18]Richardson, *op. cit.*, VIII, 301.

FIGURE 53. USE OF *op. cit.* THE WORK BY RICHARDSON HAD PREVIOUSLY BEEN CITED IN FULL [Reprinted from Manfred Jonas: *Isolationism in America*, 1935–1941. Copyright © 1966 by Cornell University. Used by permission of Cornell University Press.]

"President *and*—Not *vs.*—Congress," New York *Times Magazine,* June 20, 1948, p. 26.

5. No implications are intended at this point about individual responsibility versus party responsibility. The statement holds under either view of responsibility, although techniques for enforcing responsibility would differ.

6. These assumptions are not quite the same as either Professor Schumpeter's "classical doctrine of democracy" or his "new theory of democracy," although the theory as stated here seems to me to be more nearly in accord with reality than his. See J. A. Schumpeter, *Capitalism, Socialism, and Democracy,* 2d ed., Harper, 1947, chaps. xxi-xxii.

7. *Organization of Congress: Hearings before the Joint Committee,* 79th Cong., 1st sess., p. 281. See also Rep. Ramspeck's testimony on the same point, p. 295. The Legislative Reorganization Act of 1946 provided for adjournment by the end of July. In 1948 a special session was called. In 1949 the session ran, despite the Act, through the summer and early fall.

8. Gleeck, "96 Congressmen Make Up Their Minds," pp. 14-15.

9. The American Institute of Public Opinion (AIPO), Nov. 2, 1939. An AIPO poll with slightly different wording reported on Oct. 22, 1939 that 60 per cent of the sample favored repeal and 40 per cent opposed it.

10. Rowena Wyant, "Voting Via the Senate Mailbag," *Public Opinion Quarterly,* Fall 1941, pp. 359-82, and Winter 1941, pp. 590-624. See especially pp. 360, 372-73.

11. American Institute of Public Opinion, Sept. 24, 1949. To the question, "Have you ever written or wired your Congressman or Senator in Washington?" the response was:

	Yes	No
By occupation		
Prof. and business	33%	67%
White collar	20	80
Farmers	17	83
Manual workers	12	88
By education		
College	39	61
High school	21	79
Grammar school	11	89

12. On Congressional attitudes toward mail on neutrality legislation, see Gleeck, *loc. cit.,* p. 14. For one Congressman's general attitude toward letter-writers, see Jerry Voorhis, *Confessions of a Congressman,* Doubleday, 1948, chap. v.

13. These figures may be compared with the results of a mail questionnaire in 1940 to all U.S. Senators and two hundred Representatives, to which thirty-three Senators and eighty-four Representatives replied. To the question, "Do the results of public opinion polls aid you in deciding upon the desires of your constituents?" 71 per cent replied "no." When, however,

FIGURE 54.   USE OF *loc. cit.* NOTE NO. 12 REFERS TO THE SAME PLACE IN THE SAME WORK AS NOTE NO. 8. [Robert A. Dahl, *Congress and Foreign Policy* (New York: Harcourt, Brace & World, 1950), p. 266. Used by permission of the publisher.]

Systematic Research In Experimental Phonetics:
1. A Theory Of The Speech Mechanism
As A Servosystem

Grant Fairbanks

EXPERIMENTAL phonetics is the study of the biological action known as *speaking* which produces the acoustical time-series known as *speech*. Numerous biological systems are involved in this action, but it is possible to consider them collectively as a single, larger, bio-acoustical system which is a proper object of study as such. It is this system, the *speaking system*, as a system, that I propose to discuss. While it is impractical to cite all my sources ~~I want to men~~

~~notes of a piano, but by~~ modulation as a function of time. Certain of the elements, such as the diphthongs, involve characteristic changes during their durations, losing their entities if they do not so change. Other elements, such as the vowels, may be prolonged indefinitely in the steady state and change is not considered to be a defining feature. During production of elements of the latter type in connected speech, however, changes occur. Movements to and from articulatory positions result in acoustic transitions to and from steady states in the output.

In the model we have seen how a transition is used for purposes of control and prediction. From it is derived a changing error signal. The model's objective is to reduce this error signal to zero, and at such a time as that has been accomplished the control point will have been reached. In the case of the production of elements of

By way of review I will first show without discussion five diagrams of communication systems. Figure 1 is from Scripture (*5*), Figure 2 from Shannon (*6*), Figure 3 from Davis (*2*), and Figure 4 from Peterson (*4*). Figure 5 shows Bott's (*1*) unpublished *speaker-listener causal series*, which has been passed on by word of mouth. As nearly as I can determine, it must have been formulated about 1930, antedating the four others. The diagram, which shows only structural

References

1. Bott, E. A. (Indirect personal communication)
2. Davis, H. Auditory communication. *JSHD*, 16, 1951, 3-8.
3. MacColl, L. A. *Fundamental Theory of Servomechanisms*. New York: D. Van Nostrand, 1945.
4. Peterson, G. E. Basic physical systems for communication between two individuals. *JSHD*, 18, 1953, 116-120.
5. Scripture, E. W. Der Mechanismus der Sprachsysteme. Z. *Experimentalphonetik*, 1, 1931, 85-90.
6. Shannon, C. E. and W. Weaver. *The Mathematical Theory of Communication*. Urbana: Univ. of Ill. Press, 1949.
7. Trimmer, J. D. The basis for a science of instrumentology. *Science*, 118, 1953, 461-465.
8. ———. *Response of Physical Systems*. New York: Wiley, 1950.
9. Wiener, N. *Cybernetics*. New York: Wiley, 1948.
10. ———. *The Human Use of Human Beings*. Boston: Houghton Mifflin, 1950.

FIGURE 55.   USE OF TERMINAL NOTES [Reprinted from *Experimental Phonetics: Selected Articles*, edited by Grant Fairbanks (Urbana: University of Illinois Press, 1966) pp. 3, 9. By permission of the University of Illinois Press and the *Journal of Speech and Hearing Disorders*.]

BIBLIOGRAPHIC STYLE

Consistency

There are few universal rules governing the form of bibliographies and footnotes. Much is left to the taste and judgment of the author. For this reason it is especially important that he take care to be consistent in order to avoid misleading his reader. Faced with the title page pictured in Figure 56, for example, the author must make certain decisions. Should the authors' names be arranged thus:

Gregory, James S. and Shave, D. W.

or thus:

Gregory, James S. and D. W. Shave?

A minor consideration, perhaps, but one which could lead to confusion unless a consistent pattern is established. He must also decide whether he intends to include with the authors' names such titles as "formerly Geography Master, Trinity School, Middlesex" and whether he wants to search out the authors' full names or to settle for initials. Does he want to set a precedent for listing complete titles (*The U.S.S.R.; A Geographical Survey*), or will the short title (*The U.S.S.R.*) be sufficient? Should he cite the publisher as "John Wiley & Sons, Inc., or simply as "Wiley"? How does he indicate that the date of publication, which he has found elsewhere, does not appear on the title page? A good style manual can help him establish a consistent form. (Several such manuals are listed at the end of this chapter.)

Variations

These manuals do not, however, always agree among themselves, for bibliographic practice differs from one discipline to another. Compare, for example, the different styles which the same reference might assume in the following journals:

THE U.S.S.R.

A Geographical Survey

BY

JAMES S. GREGORY B.A. F.R.G.S.

FORMERLY GEOGRAPHY MASTER TRINITY COUNTY SCHOOL MIDDLESEX

AND

D. W. SHAVE M.Sc.

SENIOR GEOGRAPHY MASTER TRINITY COUNTY SCHOOL MIDDLESEX
LECTURER IN GEOGRAPHY METHOD WESTMINSTER TRAINING COLLEGE LONDON

NEW YORK

JOHN WILEY & SONS, Inc.

FIGURE 56. A TITLE PAGE [James S. Gregory and D. W. Shave, *The U.S.S.R.: A Geographical Survey* (New York: John Wiley & Sons, Inc.,© 1944). Used by permission of the publisher.]

JOURNAL	REFERENCE
Psychological Reports	Davis, Allen F. Welfare, reform, and World War I. *American Quarterly*, 1967, 19, 516–533.
American Literature	Davis, Allen F. "Welfare, Reform, and World War I" *American Quarterly*, XIX, 516–33 (Fall, 1967).
American Anthropologist	Davis, Allen F. 1967 Welfare, reform, and World War I. American Quarterly 19:516–533.
American Sociological Review	Davis, A. F. 1967 "Welfare, reform, and World War I." American Quarterly 19 (Fall): 516–533.

In some cases the preferred bibliographic style has been codified as, for example, in the *MLA Style Sheet*[10] and in the *Publication Manual* of the American Psychological Association.[11] The preferred style for any discipline may usually be discovered by studying the practice of its leading journals and their bibliographic instructions to contributors. However, many questions of bibliographic style will have to be decided by the author. His best guides are his knowledge of his subject, of his potential readers, and of the purpose of citation, namely, to enable the reader to identify and locate the source with a minimum chance of error.

No niceties of bibliographic style, however, can take the place of careful, accurate description. The scrambled title, the blind footnote, the "ghost" reference, the careless proofreading are not unknown in scholarly writing. Patience, thoroughness, and accuracy are some of a scholar's virtues. Bibliography, a part of the scholar's equipment, calls upon him to practice them strenuously.

---

[10]Modern Language Association of America, *The MLA Style Sheet*, rev. ed. (New York: Modern Language Association, 1951).

[11]American Psychological Association, *Publication Manual*, rev. 1967 (Washington: American Psychological Association, 1967).

THE USES OF BIBLIOGRAPHY

Bibliography takes many forms. It may list and describe current publications within a particular country, or concern itself with a retrospective record of publishing. It may concentrate on the publications of a government, whether local or national, or on the records of an international body. It may bring together from many sources the writings on a given subject, or thread the maze of scholarly publication. From the beginning the purpose of bibliography has been to create a meaningful order among the records of human experience. For those whose work is concerned with these records a knowledge of the forms and conventions of bibliography becomes a necessity, for bibliography is the line which links scholar to scholar across political boundaries and opens the heritage of the past to scholars of the present and the future.

SUGGESTIONS FOR FURTHER INVESTIGATION

I. Is there a manual of bibliographic style for your discipline? If so, identify it. If not, you may want to write one, based on the usage of the leading journals of your field.
II. Using the bibliographic style appropriate to your discipline, write a documented paper on a subject related to bibliography.

References for the preceding problems

Campbell, William Giles, *Form and Style in Thesis Writing*. Rev. ed. Boston: Houghton Mifflin Company, 1954.

Hurt, Peyton, *Bibliography and Footnotes*. Rev. ed. Berkeley: University of California Press, 1949.

Turabian, Kate L., *A Manual for Writers of Term Papers, Theses, and Dissertations*. 3d. ed. Chicago: University of Chicago Press, 1967.

Winchell, Constance M., *Guide to Reference Books*. 8th ed. Chicago: American Library Association, 1967; *First Supplement, 1965–1966.* Chicago: American Library Association, 1968.

¹Translated by Ralph R. Shaw (New York: Columbia University Press, 1934), p. 35.

INDEX